Beading with Cabochons

Beading with Cabochons

Simple Techniques for Beautiful Jewelry

Jamie Cloud Eakin

LARK
CRAFTS

An Imprint of Sterling Publishing Co., Inc.
New York

WWW.LARKCRAFTS.COM

Dedicated to
Stephen and Candace

Editor: Terry Krautwurst
Art Directors: Stacey Budge (photography) and 828, Inc. (layout)
Cover Designer: Barbara Zaretsky
Photographer: Steve Mann
Illustrator: Orrin Lundgren
Assistant Editor: Susan Kieffer
Associate Art Director: Shannon Yokeley
Editorial Assistance: Delores Gosnell
Art Production Assistance: Jeffrey Hamilton
Art Intern: Emily Kepley

Library of Congress Cataloging-in-Publication Data

Eakin, Jamie Cloud.
  Beading with cabochons : simple techniques for beautiful jewelry / Jamie
Cloud Eakin.
     p. cm.
  Includes index.
  ISBN 1-57990-718-0 (hardcover)
  1. Beadwork. 2. Jewelry making. I. Title.
  TT860.E25 2005
  745.594'2--dc22
                              2005014242

10 9 8

Published by Lark Crafts, an Imprint of Sterling Publishing Co., Inc.
387 Park Avenue South, New York, N.Y. 10016

Distributed in Canada by Sterling Publishing,
c/o Canadian Manda Group, 165 Dufferin Street
Toronto, Ontario, Canada M6K 3H6

Distributed in the United Kingdom by GMC Distribution Services,
Castle Place, 166 High Street, Lewes, East Sussex, England BN7 1XU

Distributed in Australia by Capricorn Link (Australia) Pty Ltd.,
P.O. Box 704, Windsor, NSW 2756 Australia

If you have questions or comments about this book, please contact:
Lark Crafts
67 Broadway
Asheville, NC 28801
(828) 253-0467

Manufactured in China

ISBN 13: 978-1-57990-718-1

For information about custom editions, special sales, premium and corporate purchases, please contact Sterling Special Sales Department at 800-805-5489 or specialsales@sterlingpub.com.

For information about desk and examination copies available to college and university professors, requests must be submitted to academic@larkbooks.com. Our complete policy can be found at www.larkcrafts.com.

table of contents

Introduction	6
Chapter 1 - MATERIALS AND TOOLS	8
Chapter 2 - BASIC CABOCHON BEADING	15
Chapter 3 - EDGE STITCHES	23
Chapter 4 - ATTACHMENT METHODS	46
Chapter 5 - OTHER BEZEL STITCHES	60
Chapter 6 - THE PROJECTS	69
Fringed Dichroic Glass Necklace	70
Oval Solitaire Rhodonite Bracelet	74
Noondrite Jasper Necklace	77
Sea Moss Ladder Bracelet	80
Double Cabochon Dangle Earrings	84
Leopardskin Jasper Necklace	88
Black Onyx Pin	91
Victorian Triple Cabochon Bracelet	93
Southwest Spirit Necklace	96
Fringed Tiger-Eye Cabochon Earrings	99
Crazy Lace Agate Pin	102
Chapter 7 - CREATING YOUR OWN DESIGNS	104
Gallery	112
Appendix - ATTACHING FINDINGS	118
Index to Stitches	125
A Note About Suppliers	126

introduction

I BELIEVE THAT BEADS ARE ONE OF THE MOST seductive materials that artists and crafters have ever encountered. I also believe that, for many (and I'm one of them!), lovely stone or glass cabochons come in a close second. Both beads and cabochons offer amazing variety, dazzling beauty, and virtually unlimited creative possibilities. Combine the two in a single form—beading with cabochons—and those possibilities become boundless.

I wouldn't be surprised, then, to find out that you're reading this book because you, too, have been seduced by beads or cabochons or both. Perhaps you're a beader who, one day while out bead shopping, came across a cabochon that you loved and just had to buy—even though you had no clear notion of what you might do with it. Or maybe you've simply seen a piece of spectacular cabochon beadwork and have been inspired by it.

Regardless of your motivation, you'll discover in this book everything you need to turn that motivation into a rewarding creative endeavor—and perhaps a full-time passion.

In the first several chapters, you'll learn a variety of techniques and methods for creating stunning cabochon beadwork. Although you may recognize some of the stitches from basic bead embroidery, this book

shows you how to adapt them for cabochon beading. Others are unique stitches that I developed specifically for cabochon beadwork, integrated into a process that I developed over more than a decade of experience. Each technique is detailed with illustrations and step-by-step instructions so that even beginners will be comfortable learning. Numerous photographs of beaded cabochon jewelry also are included, to inspire you and to show you examples of the many ways you can apply the techniques you're learning.

Immediately following the techniques chapters, you'll find specific step-by-step instructions for a variety of jewelry projects to make as you develop and hone your cabochon beading skills. The projects range from simple (such as a single-strand rose-pink bracelet and a pair of double-cabochon earrings) to more complicated endeavors (such as an elaborately fringed dichroic glass necklace and a leopardskin jasper necklace with a spiraling black-and-gold twisted edge). Each project includes a complete list of the beads and other materials and supplies you need to create a piece like the one shown. And the jewelry projects themselves are indeed beautiful; each is truly a work of wearable art. But don't let the lists fool you into thinking that you're limited to making just the projects exactly as shown in the photographs.

The wonderful thing about beading with cabochons is that every item you make is truly one-of-a-kind. Whether it's a polished natural stone or an artist's fused-glass creation, a cabochon is unique. So although you can count the projects included here on your fingers and toes, you can create a nearly infinite number of variations just by changing the cabochon and the bead colors while using the same project instructions. Your creation can be earthy, rich, and dark, or you can make it bright, colorful, and whimsical. Even the simplest cabochon beadwork design can be done and redone, again and again, yet each is unique, with its own personality. If you take a closer look, too, at all of the example photos in the techniques chapters, you'll find that each is captioned with a list of the techniques used in the piece—so, in effect, each of those pieces also is a project waiting to be made with your own special touches.

It won't take you long before you discover that the greatest satisfaction—and joy—of beading with cabochons comes from creating your own designs,

> "The wonderful thing about beading with cabochons is that every item you make is truly one-of-a-kind."

from the never-ending process of learning how to adapt techniques and materials to the particular properties of a particular cabochon and the vision you have for it. So in the chapter following the projects, I've included a wealth of design advice and information to help you explore the unlimited creative territory beyond this book.

Like many people, I did beadwork as a child and returned to it with a passion as an adult. I studied, experimented, and tried to master every stitch I saw. And then one day I saw a beaded necklace with a stone cabochon as the focal point. I was awestruck; I knew at that moment I had found the form of expression and creative pursuit I was longing for. Now, over a decade later, I can tell you that the studying, experimenting, and striving for mastery never end. There is always more to accomplish and learn; you are never really done.

Whether you are at that "master" stage of beading or are a complete novice, my sincere wish is that the methods and techniques you find here will help you on your own wondrous journey.

materials and tools

Part of the lure of beading with cabochons is that it allows you to make beautiful, unique, professional-looking jewelry and other creations, yet the techniques are remarkably simple. Gather together just a few materials and tools, and you're on your way.

Cabochons

A *cabochon* is a stone, gem, or other object that has a flat back and a smooth dome surface. The material can be either natural (such as agate) or man-made (such as glass). Cabochons come in many shapes and sizes, from very small, such as 5 mm rounds, to large, such as 30 x 40 mm ovals. Lapidaries love to use the cabochon shape because the polished dome surface is perfect for highlighting a stone's colors and variations. Glass and ceramic artists have also discovered the advantages of using this simple shape to create lovely little pieces of art.

Cabochons are widely available on the Web and in most local bead shops. Rock and gem shows are another great place to find cabochons and offer the added advantage of a fun shopping experience. These shows are advertised on the Web and in many bead and lapidary magazines. With all the materials now used to make cabochons, you can find any color your heart desires!

For your first projects, I recommend that you choose either round or oval cabochons with a dome that's approximately 4 mm high and that has a good slope tapering to a thin edge. This shape and configuration is easiest to bead properly. After you've become comfortable with the basic techniques of cabochon beadwork, you can expand the universe of your selections to include stones with odd shapes, flattened domes, or thick edges.

Beads

Technically, a bead is defined as anything with a hole in it that can be strung, woven, embroidered, or otherwise assembled with other beads to create jewelry or some other object.

In cabochon beadwork, the cabochon is surrounded by rows of beads stitched around its outside edge to a backing material. The initial row around the outside edge is called the *base row*. In the techniques described in this book, an additional row of beads,

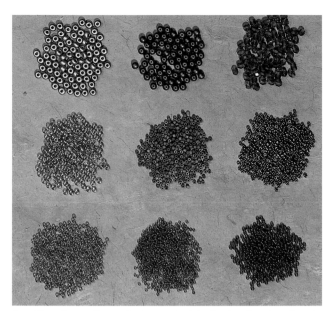

Seed beads are the mainstay material of cabochon beadwork. They're available in an array of finishes, from matte to metallic, and in an almost unlimited spectrum of colors.

called the *bezel*, encircle the face just inside the base row to hold the stone in place.

Round beads work best for all of these rows because their curves allow them to lie more perfectly next to one another and follow the curvature of the cabochon. Cylindrical beads are not well suited for the cabochon rows, but they are useful for other design elements in your creations.

Round *seed beads*, small glass beads named for the seeds they resemble, are commonly used for the beaded rows. These beads are also referred to as rocailles. Seed beads are sized according to number; the higher the number, the smaller the bead. (The number is usually followed by what looks like a degree mark, as in size 13°, or by a slash and the number 0, as in 13/0. This book uses the degree-mark approach.) Many other kinds of beads are sized in millimeters.

Most cabochon beadwork projects will use size 11° and/or size 15° to bead around the cabochon and create the bezel. In chapter five, Other Bezel Stitches, various other bead sizes—such as size 5° or 6° (large seed beads called "E" beads), or 3 mm to 8 mm beads—are used either for creative

effects or to solve particular problems related to the curve of the cabochon. Be cautious of some Czech seed beads, especially sizes 13° and smaller, because many of those beads have very small holes. Japanese seed beads work well because they generally have larger holes and are uniform in size. Beads with larger holes give you more design options because you can pass needle and thread through the bead many times.

Actually, any bead can be used in cabochon beadwork, with the provision that the hole in the bead be large enough to allow passing the needle and thread through it at least four times. Many of the stitches in this book require the needle and thread to pass through the beads several times, so if the hole is not large enough you're likely to encounter problems completing a stitch. If you're not sure the beads you want to use for a piece have sufficiently large holes, test them first. This hole-size criterion excludes very few beads. In other words, your choices for cabochon beadwork are nearly unlimited.

Beading needles and thread

Needles and Threads

The needles and threads used in cabochon beadwork are made specifically for beading. Needles come in sizes 10, 12, 13, 15, and 16; the higher the number, the smaller the needle. For the projects in this

Knots

Throughout this book, you'll be instructed to tie knots. The good news is that you need to know how to tie only two basic kinds, and they're both easy to learn—in fact, you may already be familiar with them.

Square Knot Steps

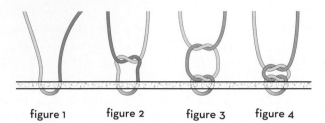

figure 1   figure 2   figure 3   figure 4

Square Knot

This is the preferred knot to use whenever you need to join two threads or two thread ends. The important quality of a square knot is that it tightens on itself when the ends are pulled; some knots actually loosen instead. To tie a square knot, position the thread ends that you want to join so that one is to the right and the other is to the left (figure 1). Loop the right over and around the left (figure 2). Then take the thread that is now on the left and loop it over and around the right (figure 3). Pull the ends to secure the knot (figure 4).

Be sure to weave in the ends before you cut so that you are not cutting next to the knot. This includes the situation where you are tying off a stitch that is worked double-thread. In that case, cut the thread near the needle and put a needle on the other thread end, too. Take one of the needles and stitch over ⅛ inch (3 mm) to provide a base between the two threads; then tie the knot. This is more secure than tying the knot where both threads are coming out of the same hole, because a knot in that situation could be pulled down into the hole.

One-Thread Knot

This knot is useful whenever you have only one thread end and therefore can't tie a square knot. Stitch down into the fabric to create a small loop (figure 5). Be sure to grab enough fabric so that the knot is anchored securely. Pass the needle and thread through the loop twice and pull (figures 6 and 7). The trick to this knot is to manage the thread so that the loops are small before you pull to tighten. If there's going to be a lot of stress (pull) on the knot, stitch over and do a second knot. Be sure to weave in the end before you cut so that you are not cutting next to the knot.

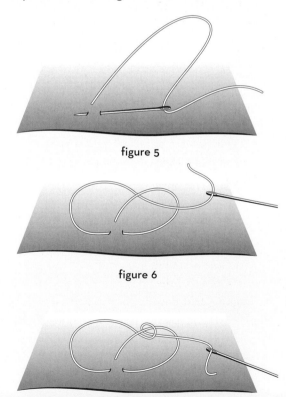

figure 5

figure 6

figure 7

book, you'll need a beading needle size 12 or 13. English-made beading needles tend to have a larger hole for the thread in relation to the circumference of the needle than other types; in other words, the needles are thinner and easier to thread. Beading threads come in various materials, colors, and sizes. For cabochon beadwork, I recommend pre-waxed, twisted multifilament beading thread in size A. This type of thread is available in nylon fibers and rice fibers. Unwaxed, untwisted multifilament thread in size A or B also can be used, but it needs to be waxed and tends to fray more than the other type when the thread is drawn through fabric backing many times. You can minimize this fraying by rewaxing the thread periodically while you're beading.

In this book's instructions, some methods call for working a project *single-thread* and others *double-thread*. To work double-thread, simply move the needle to the center of the thread so that you have two equal-length strands.

tip:

Threading Problems?
You Are Not Alone!
Threading a beading needle is a challenge for everyone. Practice and experience will make you more comfortable with this essential part of beading. Don't get discouraged.

Backing Materials

Cabochon beadwork employs two separate layers of backing material—an under backing, to which the cabochon is glued and the initial rows sewn on, and an outer backing that covers the stitched material and serves as the piece's visible back. Under backing material needs to be sturdy, with a composition that doesn't fray when cut. I recommend the special beading foundation material sold in many beading stores and on the Internet. The product is made specifically for cabochon beading and other bead embroidery techniques. It is lightweight yet has a sturdy body to support even very heavy beads and is excellent for holding its shape.

You can also use other materials for under backing, such as heavy interfacing material available at fabric stores. Choose fusible interfacing and increase the material's stability by fusing two pieces together with an iron. Other options for under backing material include leather, suede, synthetic suede, and felt. All these materials can be cut without fraying. However, they don't hold their shape as well as beading foundation material and may be more difficult to push a needle through.

Although the under backing isn't clearly visible on a finished piece, there may be small areas between the beads that show through. Accordingly, it is appropriate to use a color that blends into the background. You can use permanent markers and/or acrylic paints to color materials that are available only in white. It's not necessary to match the color of the beads or cabochons, but simply to tone down the bright white of these products. You can buy leather and synthetic suede in a variety of colors or tint them yourself.

Backing materials are sold in most beading stores. Special beading foundation material (white sheet on bottom) is best for an under backing. Synthetic suede (other sheets) is a good choice for an outer backing.

I recommend using synthetic suede for the outer backing material. It's widely available in fabric stores and on the Internet. Be sure to select a synthetic suede fabric that is fused fibers and not a texture on a weave or a knit. Because the outer backing is not visible except from the back, you can use either a color that matches your beads or a neutral color.

Glue

This book focuses on techniques that create a bezel and therefore hold the cabochon in with beadwork, not with glue. However, glue is used in a temporary way, to keep the cabochon in place on the under backing while the beads are applied. This simply makes constructing the piece easier. An odor-free, flexible "tacky" glue, such as that sold in most craft stores, is sufficient.

In some instances, you may need a glue to function as the primary element that holds the cabochon in. Select a strong, heavy-duty glue that's suitable for fabric, glass, and/or stones, and that dries clear and flexible (such as rubber cement) rather than hardens. Hardware stores are a good place to look for such products.

The key to selecting one glue brand over another is knowing what the glue's texture will be after it dries. Glues that dry to a hard, inflexible surface are not appropriate because you cannot pierce it with a needle. Rather, glues that dry flexible and allow a needle to be pushed through work well.

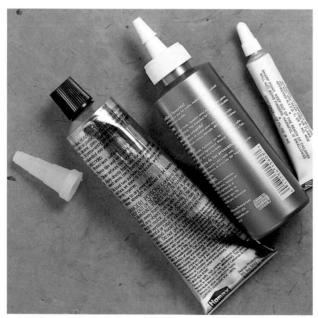

Glue types that come in handy for cabochon beadwork include general craft cement with a precision applicator (top), flexible glue (middle), and heavy-duty contact adhesive (bottom).

Findings

Findings are the ready-made fasteners and attachments—clips, clasps, pins, rings, chains, and more—that you add to beadwork to make jewelry. Most bead stores carry a vast variety of such hardware in metals ranging from inexpensive plated brass to more costly sterling silver and gold. For the projects in this book, you'll need only a few basic types (you'll find instructions for attaching findings to beaded cabochons starting on page 46).

Jump rings are useful for attaching findings to beadwork—a clasp to a beaded necklace strand, for instance.

JUMP RINGS

Jump rings are small wire circles used to link beadwork to some other kind of finding, such as a necklace clasp. The ring has a slit that can be opened. You open the ring, string it

figure 8

though the loop on the clasp and the loop on the beadwork, and then close the ring. Be careful not to open a jump ring by simply spreading the ends outward, enlarging the circle; you'll weaken the ring. Instead, using two pairs of pliers, twist the ring open, forcing one end forward and one end back (figure 8).

CLASPS

Clasps are the devices that let you open or close necklaces and bracelets. They're sold in dozens of styles and types. Some, such as lobster-claw clasps, have moving parts that allow you to shut the clasp over the attaching ring or chain on the piece's opposite end. Others, such as toggle clasps and hook clasps, simply open and close by slipping the finding through the ring or over a loop.

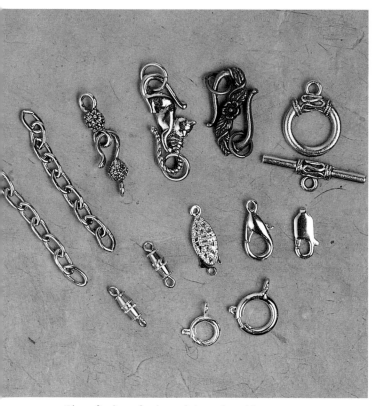

Clasp findings for bracelets and necklaces

EARRING FINDINGS

Posts, wires, and clips—most of the types that you see on commercial earrings are available to beaders, too. Some kinds have a loop that can simply be opened and closed over the beaded portion to attach it. Others have a closed loop that you must string onto the work itself to attach it. For instructions on methods for attaching earring findings to cabochons, see page 119 in the Appendix.

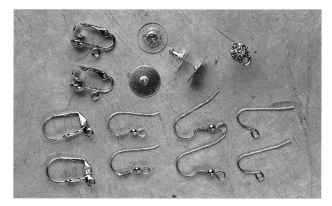

Earring findings come in three basic types: post-and-pad, dangle wires, and clasps.

PIN FINDINGS

Tie-tack-style pin findings are ideal for small pins, but bar pin findings are probably the best choice for most pins and brooches. Stickpin findings are also available with small pads at the top that are perfect for using with cabochon beadwork. For instructions on methods for attaching pin findings to cabochons, see page 122 in the Appendix.

Pin findings, from left: tie-tack style, bar pins, and stickpin

tip:

Invest in Quality

Whether it's tools or materials, always buy the best you can afford. Quality tools may cost more initially, but they will save you time and money in the long run. The same is true of good beads and findings. You'll put a lot of time and effort into your pieces, and quality materials will help ensure that you'll be proud of your work in every aspect.

tip:

Light Up Your Workplace

Seed beads are small, so good lighting is essential for a pleasurable beading experience. Be sure to light your workplace sufficiently. There are special beading lamps available that have the added benefit of providing a "true color" light, which helps you select the right color beads. These lamps also usually give off less heat than regular lamps. They're available at craft shops, office supply stores, and bead shops, and on the Internet.

Tools

Chances are good that you already have all the tools you'll need to start beading with cabochons.

PLIERS

Needle nose or round nose pliers are useful for opening and closing jump rings and for such tasks as attaching ear wires to beadwork. It is helpful to have two pairs of pliers so that you can have one in each hand to open and close a jump ring. These types of pliers are available in most bead shops and hardware stores.

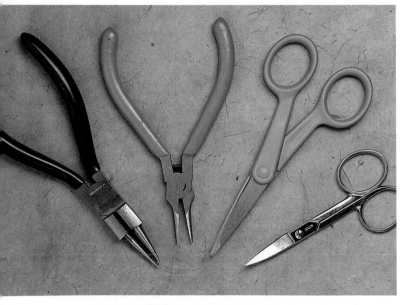

Scissors and pliers are the only real tools you'll need.

SCISSORS

Good, sharp blades and a small size for easy maneuverability is my description of great scissors to use for beadwork. Craft shops, fabric stores, and bead shops all have good scissors to add to your beadwork tool chest. I like to use small curved manicure scissors to trim the backings on round or oval cabochons. The curve of the scissors makes the trimming job easier. These are readily available at drugstores.

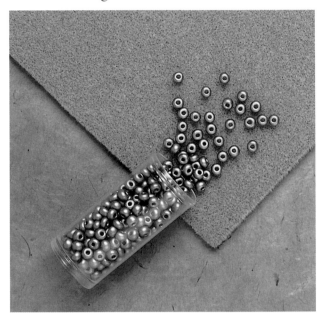

A beading pad keeps beads from rolling around every which way and makes picking beads up with a needle easier.

BEADING PAD

Made specifically for beading, these pads resemble a small fleece blanket with a nap like that of velvet. The fabric provides a cushioned surface, allowing you to pour out small piles of beads to use without them rolling all over the place. Instead, the beads sit on top of the nap fibers and are easy to pick up with a needle. Beading pads are available at most bead stores and on the Internet. Or, as a substitute, you can use a folded kitchen towel (the woven type without loops).

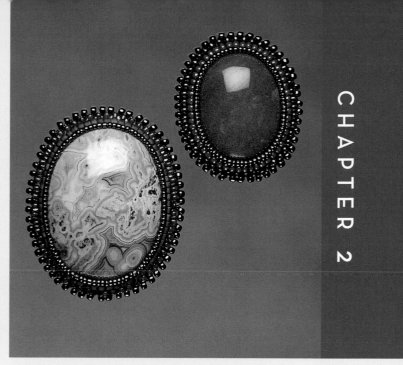

CHAPTER 2

Cabochon: **Black onyx**
Bezel: **Standard**
Edge: **Pointed with tassel**
Attachment: **Direct**

Cabochon: **Ruby in zoisite**
Bezel: **Standard**
Edge: **Pointed, fringed, raw**
Attachment: **Turn bead**

Cabochons: **Crazy lace agate, Indian agate**
Bezel: **Standard**
Edge: **Picot edge variation**

basic cabochon beading

This chapter includes all of the techniques necessary to bead a base row, a bezel, and any of several kinds of edges. The end result: a dazzling basic beaded cabochon to use as the focal point for a necklace, bracelet, earrings, pin, or other jewelry design.

The Process

There are six steps to creating a basic beaded cabochon: 1) attach the cabochon to the under backing material, 2) bead the base row, 3) add the bezel row, 4) attach the outer backing, 5) bead the edge, and 6) mark the center beads.

WHAT YOU NEED:

Cabochon (see Note)

Scissors

Piece of under backing material

Flexible glue

Round seed beads, size 11° or 12° (for base and edge rows)

Round seed beads, size 14° or 15° (for bezel row)

Beading needles, size 12 or 13

Beading thread, size A

Piece of outer backing material

Piece of white paper

Dark ink pen

Note: Unless you're an experienced cabochon beader, choose a round or oval cabochon with a nice dome (not flattened) that slopes all the way to a thin edge rather than a rounded or blunt edge. In later chapters, you'll learn other stitches and techniques to use with nonstandard cabochon shapes.

Step One:

Attach the Cabochon to the Under Backing

A. With scissors, cut a piece of under backing that's larger than the cabochon by at least ½ inch (1.3 cm) on all sides. Apply an even layer of glue to the cabochon's back and press it firmly against the backing material. Let the glue dry thoroughly. Remember, the glue's purpose is solely to hold the cabochon in place while you're beading. Because a permanent bond is not necessary, you can use almost any type of glue. I prefer flexible craft glue.

Step Two:

Bead the Base Row

The first row you'll be beading will actually be the second row from the center of the finished cabochon. Use size 11° or 12° seed beads in whichever color you want for this second-from-the-center row. You'll use a bead embroidery stitch called a backstitch. This particular type is referred to as the "four-six backstitch" because you add four beads and then stitch back six beads.

A. Thread a needle with approximately 2 yards (1.83 m) of beading thread (this row is worked single-thread).

tip:

Be Generous with Your Thread
Always start beading with a generous length of thread. It usually takes more time and effort to add another piece of thread than to work with a long thread.

B. Bring the needle up from the underside of the backing with the needle inserted as close as possible to the edge of the cabochon. Leave a tail thread in the back that's approximately 9 inches (22.9 cm) long. Don't tie a knot at the end of the thread; just leave the tail loose. Now pick up four size 11° or 12° beads and stitch down through the backing, leaving enough room for the four added beads (figure 1).

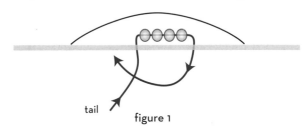

tail   figure 1

C. Bring the needle back toward the starting point of the first stitch and push the needle back up through the backing, leaving room to add two beads between the point where the needle entered and the four beads already added. Pick up two beads and pass the needle through the four beads, creating a six-bead row (figure 2).

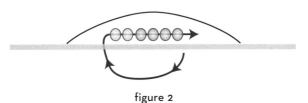

figure 2

tip:

Leave Room for Added Beads
When you're adding beads with the backstitch, be sure to leave plenty of room for the beads when you stitch forward. If you stitch too close, the added beads will bow upward from the backing and create problems with later stitching. In contrast, if you leave enough room—or even too much room—later stitches will still work well. The moral here is, when stitching, err on the side of too long instead of too short.

D. Next, pick up four beads and stitch down into the backing next to the edge of the cabochon, leaving enough room for the four new beads. From the back side, bring the needle back up to the top side, counting back six beads. As always, the needle should be inserted next to the edge of the cabochon. Now, from the top, bring the needle through the six beads (figure 3).

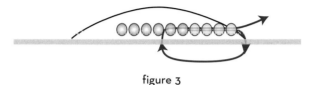

figure 3

E. Repeat this process, adding four beads and stitching back six, around the cabochon, until you reach a point where you need four or fewer beads to complete the circle.

F. To close the loop, change the stitch to suit the number of beads you need to add to fill the remaining space.

- Need four beads to close: Pick up only two beads (instead of four) and go back only four beads (instead of six). Pick up two beads and proceed to G.
- Need three beads to close: Pick up only two beads and go back only four beads. Pick up one bead and proceed to G.
- Need two beads to close: Pick up only one bead and go back only three beads. Pick up one bead and proceed to G.
- Need one bead to close: Don't add any beads. Stitch down through the under backing and go back two beads. Pick up one bead and proceed to G.

G. Bring the needle and thread through the entire row of beads. Don't stitch down into the backing; just go through the beads in the row. Do this at least twice. Pull firmly on the thread, but not so tightly that you lift the beads, or so loosely that the thread leaves a loop. Continue around and around the bead row until it's too difficult to bring the needle through the beads anymore. Basically, what you're doing is filling up the holes in the beads with the thread. This will force the beads to line up straight with each other and make the row strong and firm.

H. When you've finished, stitch the needle to the back side, entering next to the edge of the cabochon. On the back side, take the needle end and stitch over to the tail end. Tie a square knot. Weave the ends in and cut.

tip:

Stay Close to the Cabochon!
When stitching around the cabochon to create the base, bezel, and additional rows, always pass the needle through the backing fabric as close as possible to the edge of the cabochon. Later, you'll use scissors to trim away excess backing material. If your stitches aren't near the edge of the cabochon, there's a risk that you'll inadvertently cut the thread.

Step Three:

Add the Bezel Row

Now it's time to create the bezel row, which holds the cabochon in place. The bezel should sit slightly above the previous row, next to the cabochon, in the "valley" between that row and the cabochon. Use size 14° or 15° seed beads in whichever color you want for this innermost row. Using smaller beads than the previous row enhances the final beaded cabochon's dome shape.

A. Thread a needle with approximately 2 yards (1.83 m) of beading thread (this row is worked single-thread).

B. For this row you'll again use a backstitch, but this time it'll be the four-two variety; in other words, you'll add four beads and then stitch back two beads. To start, bring the needle up from the back side with the needle inserted next to the edge of the cabochon, between the cabochon and the base row of beads. Leave a tail thread in the back that's approximately 9 inches (22.9 cm) long. Don't tie a knot; just leave the tail end loose. Add four size 14° or 15° beads onto the needle and thread. Bring the needle down through the under backing, leaving room for the four added beads. Make sure that the beads sit in the channel between the cabochon and the row previously sewn on, and that they *sit up* in this channel comfortably; don't pull down and wedge them in between the cabochon and the row previously sewn on, and don't pull the stitch so tight that it moves the previous row. Let the beads sit on top (figure 4).

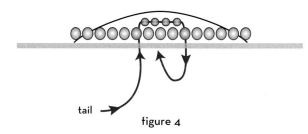

tail

figure 4

tip:

Watch That Needle

As you're working on a piece and adding new stitches, don't let the needle pierce the threads from previous stitches. This can create problems with how the beads will lie, and it weakens the construction.

C. Now bring the needle back up to the top, counting two beads backward, and through the last two added beads (figure 5). As always, the needle should enter next to the edge of the cabochon, inside of the first row of beads.

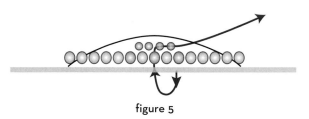

figure 5

D. Continue with the four-two backstitch around the cabochon (figure 6).

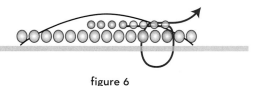

figure 6

E. When you reach a point where you need four or fewer beads to complete the circle, close the loop by changing the stitch to suit the number of beads you need to add to fill the remaining space.

- Need four beads to close: Pick up three beads (instead of four) and go back two beads. Add one bead and proceed to F.
- Need three beads to close: Pick up two beads (instead of four) and go back one bead. Add one bead and proceed to F.
- Need two beads to close: Pick up two beads and proceed to F.
- Need one bead to close: Pick up one bead and proceed to F.

F. Bring the needle and thread through the entire row of beads. Don't go down into the backing; just go through the beads in the row. Do this at least twice. Pull firmly on the thread, but not so tightly that you lift the beads or so loosely that the thread leaves a loop. Continue around and around the bead row until it's too difficult to bring the needle through the beads anymore. Basically, what you're doing is filling up the holes in the beads with the thread. This will force the beads to line up straight with each other and make the row strong and firm.

G. When you've finished, bring the needle down through the backing to the back side, entering next to the edge of the cabochon. On the back side, take the needle end and stitch over to the tail end. Tie a square knot. Weave in the ends and cut the thread.

figure 7

H *(optional).* At this point, you can add more outer rows (beading rows around the base row) to your cabochon, using the four-two backstitch to apply the beads. Add as many as your design dictates. Do this before proceeding to the next step, in which you'll trim the under backing and add the outer backing.

Cross Section
figure 8

Step Four:

Attach the Outer Backing

Once you've finished beading the bezel row, base row, and any additional four-two backstitched rows, you'll be ready to trim the cabochon and attach the outer backing. This additional backing covers the previous stitching and combines with the under backing to provide a sturdy layer of material on which to stitch edges and decorative embellishments.

A. Using a sharp pair of scissors, trim all excess material from around the under backing. The trim line is the outer edge of the beads on the outside bead row. Be careful: Don't trim too close! It's important that you don't cut any of the threads you used to apply the beads. Remember, you can always cut off more, but you can never "uncut" if you've trimmed away too much (figures 7 and 8).

B. Now it's time to attach the outer backing material. Apply flexible glue to the center of the back of the trimmed cabochon, out to the thread lines. Don't apply glue all the way out to the edge because later on you'll need to stitch through the backings near the edge to add more beads. You don't want glue in that area. Let the glue dry.

C. Use scissors to trim the excess outer backing so that it's exactly the same size as the trimmed under backing. Be careful not to cut any more of the under backing.

Step Five:
Bead the Basic Edge

This is the last beading step in creating a basic beaded cabochon. This process will stitch the outer backing to the under backing and put one more row of beads onto the cabochon.

The basic edge stitch is similar to the blanket stitch used in embroidery, but it has a bead added to it (figure 9).

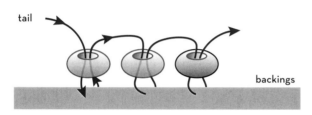

tail

backings

figure 9

A. Thread a needle with approximately 2 yards (1.83 m) of beading thread (this edge is worked single-thread).

B. Pick up one bead on the needle. Starting from the front, stitch down through the under backing and outer backing near the edge. Try to stitch with the needle entering between two beads on the outside row so that you can catch at least $1/16$ inch (1.6 mm) inside the edge of the backings. Be careful not to pierce any threads that are already there.

C. Now come up through the added bead, pulling out from the center of the cabochon, like a ray of sunshine (see the Tip above), to tighten the thread. Leave a tail of approximately 9 inches (22.9 cm).

tip:

"Like a Ray of Sunshine"
I tell my beading students to picture a child's drawing of a sun, with rays extending outward from it, when they're adding edge beads and pulling the thread to tighten it. As you pull, the line of the thread should be level with the flat surface of the cabochon back and come straight out (figure 10). Don't pull up or down (figures 11 and 12).

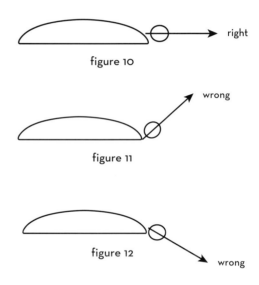

right

figure 10

wrong

figure 11

figure 12

wrong

D. Repeat steps B and C around the cabochon, moving over one bead's width for each added bead. As you near the end of closing the circle, space the added beads so there is a smooth, full closing of the circle.

E. To finish, after adding the last bead, push the needle down into the first bead before stitching down through the backings to the back side. Then take the tail end and thread a needle onto it. Push that needle down through the last added bead and stitch down through the backings to the back side (figure 13). Tie the two thread ends together with a square knot. Weave the threads into the backings and cut the ends.

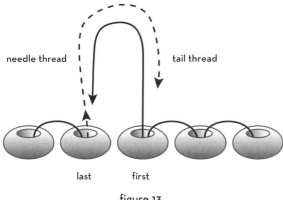

needle thread   tail thread

last   first

figure 13

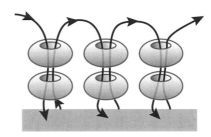

figure 14

tip:

Watch Your Spacing
The edge row should always be smooth and even.
If your edge is wavy, you're stitching the beads too
close together. The outside edges of the beads
should touch each other but should not overlap.
If there are gaps between the beads, you're stitching
the beads too far apart.

TWO-BEAD EDGE VARIATION

Once you've mastered the basic edge stitch, you can try this variation. It's a little more difficult but produces a bolder, wider edge. The stitch is the same except that you add two beads instead of one.

Just follow the same steps as above, using a second bead for each stitch (figure 14). The key to mastering the two-bead variation is to maintain the right thread tension by pulling the thread out from the bead's center, like a ray of sunshine, to tighten the thread.

There will be a wider gap between the beads on the outer row than between those on the inner row when the cabochon's edge has a curve to it. The more pronounced the curve, the wider the gap will be. Accordingly, this variation is not appropriate for cabochon shapes with corners or severe curves.

PICOT EDGE VARIATION

This variation is useful for designs, such as a simple brooch or a button earring, that will have no other edge beading. The stitch is similar to the basic edge stitch but adds a middle bead that sits sideways in the space above every two beads.

A. Follow steps A through C in the instructions for beading the basic edge.

B. Add two beads and stitch down through the backings, moving over one bead's width. As always, stitch approximately $1/16$ inch (1.6 mm) from the edge, being careful not to pierce any threads already there.

tip:

Control the Tension
The thread's tension greatly affects the look of your
beadwork. Sometimes you want a tight tension,
other times you want it loose. Whatever the case
may be, control the tension so that it's even through-
out the piece. This is a skill you'll develop as you
gain experience.

C. Bring the needle up through the second of the two added beads. The first added bead should sit sideways on top of the row (figure 15).

figure 15

D. Repeat steps B and C around the entire cabochon. As you near the end of closing the circle, space the added beads so there is a smooth, full closing of the circle.

E. To finish the edge, refer to the final step in the instructions for beading the basic edge, but add one bead to fit in the space between the last added bead and the first added bead.

tip:

How to Undo Your Mistakes

If you're not happy with a section of beading and need to undo it, always pull on the threads in the project instead of trying to retrace your steps back with the needle. If you use the needle end to undo something, you have a high probability of creating a bigger problem by piercing the threads.

Step Six:

Mark the Center Beads

Now it's time to determine how you want to position the cabochon in your creation. For example, if you have an oval cabochon, you need to decide whether you want the long axis to be vertical or horizontal. Even if you're using a round cabochon, there may be a pattern in the stone or glass that you want at the top or the bottom. Once you've made that decision, you can proceed to find the center of the top and bottom of the cabochon.

A. Put your cabochon on a blank sheet of white paper and trace around it using a dark ink pen. Hold the paper up to the light (with the light source behind the paper) and fold the sheet in half vertically while carefully matching up the outlines on both halves. Then fold it in half in the other direction, again lining up and matching the outlines, so that the tracing is folded into quarters.

B. Unfold the paper and use a pen or marker to darken the lines created by the folds. You now have an outline of your specific cabochon marked into quarters.

C. Place your cabochon on the paper. Use the lines from the folds to determine the centers of the cabochon's top, bottom, and sides. The centers will either be through the middle of a bead or between two beads. Stick a needle in the middle of each center bead or between any two beads that border a center. To double-check that you have indeed marked the actual centers, count the number of beads between the needles; the count should be the same on both sides of each needle. Reposition the needles as necessary.

D. When you're satisfied that you have the centers, tie a piece of thread around the bead (or between the two beads) of the top and bottom centers. These pieces of thread are temporary; you'll remove them later when you're sewing beads into those areas. In the meantime, they'll help you keep track of the center beads' positions.

Finished!

Congratulations; you've just completed your first beaded cabochon. Now it's time to explore additional cabochon beading techniques and to look at ways to use your creations in stunning jewelry.

edge stitches

Once you've created a basic beaded cabochon, you can take your design in many directions. This chapter illustrates a variety of finishing methods for beading on the edge row. Some edge techniques provide a simple frame to highlight that really amazing cabochon. Other edge techniques can take your design to new heights, creating a detailed artwork in which the cabochon is just one component of a complex whole.

Cabochon: **Agate**
Bezel: **Standard**
Edge: **Raw**
Attachment: **Turn bead**

Cabochon: **Carved bone**
Bezel: **Standard**
Edge: **Raw**
Attachment: **Turn bead**

Cabochon: **Striped agate**
Bezel: **Standard**
Edge: **Raw**
Attachment: **Turn bead**

Raw Edge

The raw edge technique is the easiest of them all; you're already finished! Just leave the edging on the basic beaded cabochon as it is. This is a simple, clean finish with a very tailored appearance. This edge works especially well when the thread color used to stitch the edge beads blends nicely into the color of the edge beads. Conversely, if the thread color doesn't match the beads well, the beaded cabochon can look too raw from the side because the threads will be clearly visible.

Cabochon: **Fossil stone**
Bezel: **Lifted bead**
Edge: **Turned bead**
Attachment: **Top bail ladder**

Cabochon: **Carved jadite**
Bezel: **Standard**
Edge: **Turned bead**
Attachment: **Turn bead**

Cabochon: **Turquoise**
Bezel: **Standard**
Edge: **Turned bead**
Attachment: **Turn bead**

Turned Bead Edge

This method adds one more row of beads to the outside edge of the cabochon. The effect is simple and tailored, and it has a more finished appearance than the raw edge method because no bead holes or threads show from the side of the finished piece. (The illustrations below show this edge stitch with a top bail ladder stitch attachment; see chapter four.)

INSTRUCTIONS

1. Thread a needle with approximately 2 yards (1.83 m) of beading thread (this technique is worked single-thread).

2. Insert the needle up through the top edge bead (figure 1), leaving a tail approximately 9 inches (22.9 cm) long.

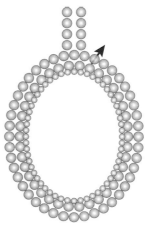

figure 1

3. Add four beads and move them into position to lie across the edge.

4. Insert the needle down into the hole of the nearest edge bead.

5. Moving backward on the added row, select the bead whose hole is under the space between bead two and bead three of the added beads. Stitch up through the hole of that bead. Then stitch through beads three and four of the added beads. Keep nudging the added beads back into their proper position (figure 2).

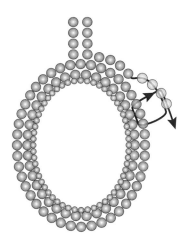

figure 3

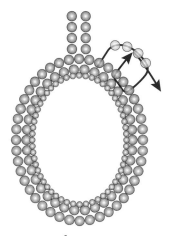

figure 2

6. Repeat steps 3 through 5 (figure 3) until the area is covered. If you need to as you near the end, adjust the count of added beads—perhaps adding only three beads, or adding five beads instead of four—in order to produce a smooth, close-fitting row.

7. Stitch through all of the added beads. Repeat, stitching through the added beads to fill the holes with thread. This will make the beads line up next to each other and smooth the appearance of the row.

8. Finally, bring the threads through the backings to the back side. Tie knots, then weave the ends in and cut.

Cabochon: **Blue lace agate**
Bezel: **Standard**
Edge: **Lifted turned bead**
Attachment: **Turn bead**

Cabochon: **Tree agate**
Bezel: **Standard**
Edge: **Lifted turned bead with points**
Attachment: **Turn bead**

Cabochon: **Simulated blueberry quartz**
Bezel: **Standard**
Edge: **Lifted turned bead**
Attachment: **Turn bead**

Lifted Turned Bead Edge

This variation of the turned bead edge lifts the added edge row out to create open spaces and an airy or lacy appearance. The method has a repeating pattern and therefore requires a count on the edge beads that is divisible by the number of beads in the repeating pattern. An alternative is to work the pattern simultaneously from each side to meet at the center of the bottom. If the beads are an even count of the pattern, you can simply join them at the meeting point. If the beads are not an even count, you can create a variation of the pattern at the bottom so that your design is still symmetrical. (The illustrations below show this edge stitch with a top bail ladder stitch attachment; see chapter four.)

INSTRUCTIONS

1. Thread a needle with approximately 2 yards (1.83 m) of beading thread (this technique is worked single-thread).

2. Insert the needle up through the top edge bead, leaving a tail approximately 9 inches (22.9 cm) long.

3. Pick up five beads.

4. Move the beads into position so that the hole of the first bead is turned in the same direction as the edge bead holes; the next three beads are turned with the holes perpendicular to the edge bead holes, and the fifth bead faces the same direction as the first.

5. Stitch into the bead directly below the fifth bead, staying on the top side. Now stitch down into the backings approximately ¹⁄₁₆ inch (1.6 mm) from the edge, and then stitch back up through the edge bead and the fifth added bead (figure 4).

figure 4

6. Pick up four beads.

7. Keeping the same spacing as in the first section, stitch down into the edge bead, staying on the top side. Now stitch down into the backings approximately ¹⁄₁₆ inch (1.6 mm) from the edge, and then stitch back up through the edge bead and the fourth added bead (figure 5).

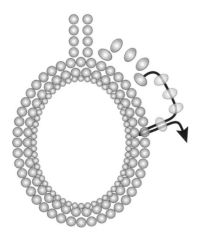

figure 5

8. Repeat steps 6 and 7 until you near the center of the bottom of the cabochon.

9. Leave the thread and start a new thread on the other side.

10. Repeat steps 1 through 8 on the other side of the cabochon.

11. Join the two sides on the bottom of the cabochon, adjusting the bead count as needed to join the sides evenly.

12. *Optional:* At this point, you can take each thread to the back side, tie a square knot, weave in the threads, and cut them to finish the piece. This will create an edge that has a somewhat scalloped appearance. Or continue with the following steps.

13. Bring the needle up through the edge bead and the added bead on top of it.

14. Go through the three turned beads. Continue around the entire edge, adding one or two beads in between each section to smooth the edge (figure 6).

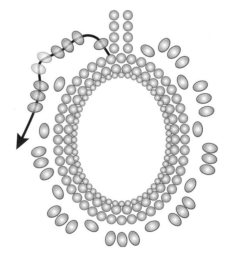

figure 6

15. Go through the outer row several times to fill the holes of the beads with thread. This will force the beads to line up straight and lie next to each other, making the row strong and firm and creating a smooth edge.

16. Finally, bring the threads to the back side. Tie them with a square knot, weave in the ends, and cut.

Variations: You can create many variations of this stitch by changing the number of added beads, and by changing bead sizes and color combinations. Each variation can create a unique appearance, but the basics of the stitch pattern are the same.

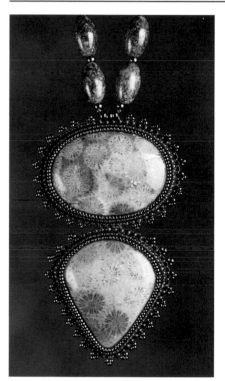

Cabochon: **Fossilized coral**
Bezel: **Standard**
Edge: **Pointed**
Attachment: **Turn bead**

Cabochon: **Serpentine**
Bezel: **Bead-raised**
Edge: **Pointed**
Attachment: **Turn bead**

Cabochon: **Amber**
Bezel: **Small cabachon variation**
Edge: **Pointed**
Attachment: **Direct**

Pointed Edge

The pointed edge method is easy to do and creates a classic, elegant look. This method has a repeating pattern and therefore requires a count on the edge beads that is divisible by two (which is the count of the repeating pattern). An alternative is to work the pattern simultaneously from each side to meet at the center of the bottom. If the beads are an even count, you can simply join at the meeting point. If the beads are not an even count, you can create a variation of the pattern at the bottom so that your design is still symmetrical. (The illustrations below show this edge stitch with a top bail ladder stitch attachment; see chapter four.)

INSTRUCTIONS

1. Thread a needle with approximately 2 yards (1.83 m) of beading thread (this technique is worked single-thread).

2. Insert the needle through the backings from the back side, approximately $^1/_{16}$ inch (1.6 mm) from the edge, leaving a tail approximately 9 inches (22.9 cm) long.

3. Stitch up through the edge bead.

4. Pick up three beads.

5. Stitch down into the next edge bead, staying on the back side (figure 7). Pull to position the beads in a triangle above the edge beads. Do not pull too tight; the middle bead of the added three beads should sit comfortably on top of the other two beads.

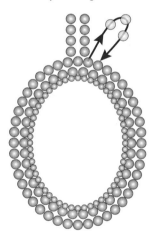

figure 7

6. Stitch back up through the first edge bead again and through the first of the three added beads.

7. Now stitch down through the third of the three added beads and the edge bead below it (skip the middle bead of the three added beads). See figure 8. Stay on the back side. Pull to adjust the three added beads into a snug triangle shape.

figure 8

8. Insert the needle into the backings approximately $^1/_{16}$ inch (1.6 mm) from the edge to bring the needle to the top side.

9. Stitch over to the next edge bead, bringing the needle through the backings approximately $^1/_{16}$ inch (1.6 mm) from the edge to the back side (figure 9).

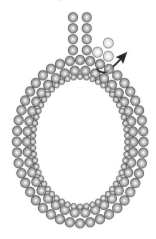

figure 9

10. Repeat steps 3 through 9 until done.

11. To finish, tie a knot in the thread, weave in the end, and cut. Add a needle to the tail thread. Tie a knot, weave in the end, and cut.

Variations: You can create a variety of appearances with this stitch by changing the size of the beads used for the points. Use size 14° or 15° for a sharp, defined edge. Use size 11° or 12° for a smoother, finished look. You can also alternate, using a size 15° for one point, then a size 11° for the next, for a staggered look.

JOINED-POINTS VARIATION

Another variation for a smoother look is to join the points together. Instead of moving to the next edge bead to start the next point, stay in the same edge bead.

A. Bring the needle through the backings and up through the same edge bead and the third added bead (figure 10).

B. Pick up two beads. Go down through the next edge bead (figure 11).

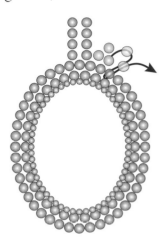

figure 11

C. Repeat steps A and B around the cabochon

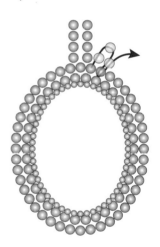

figure 10

Cabochon: **Black onyx**
Bezel: **Standard**
Edge: **Twisted**
Attachment: **Direct**

Cabochon: **Moonstone**
Bezel: **Small cabochon variation**
Edge: **Twisted**
Attachment: **Direct**

Cabochon: **Dendritic jasper**
Bezel: **Standard**
Edge: **Twisted**
Attachment: **Back side bead**

Twisted Edge

This method adds bead strands on the outside that are twisted together. You can create many different looks with the same stitch by varying the number of strands (two or three), by using tight loops or looser loops, and by using different colors in the strands. This method has a repeating pattern and therefore requires a count on the edge beads that is divisible by the length of the repeating pattern. An alternative is to work the pattern simultaneously from each side to meet at the center of the bottom. If the beads are an even count of the pattern, you can simply join at the meeting point. If the beads are not an even count, you can create a variation of the pattern at the bottom so that your design is still symmetrical. (The illustrations below show this edge stitch with a top bail ladder stitch attachment; see chapter four.)

INSTRUCTIONS

1. Thread a needle with approximately 3 yards (2.74 m) of beading thread; this method is worked double-thread, so move the needle to the center to produce a double strand.

2. Insert the needle through the backings from the back side, approximately $\frac{1}{16}$ inch (1.6 mm) from the edge, leaving a tail approximately 9 inches (22.9 cm) long.

3. Stitch up through the first edge bead.

4. Pick up one bead.

5. Stitch down into the next edge bead, staying on the back side. Pull the thread to position the bead to lie sideways between the edge beads (figure 12). This bead is referred to as the picot bead.

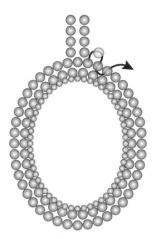

figure 12

now add beads for the first portion of the twisted strand, usually eight to 12 beads. To determine the number of beads to add for your specific cabochon and design, you will need to add some beads and test for the number it takes to produce a loop like the one in the illustration (figure 14) that extends from the first picot bead to the third picot bead. Once you have determined the number of beads to use, the same count will work for each space, unless you have severe corners or curves; then you will need to adjust the count for those areas.

6. Insert the needle into the backings approximately $^1/_{16}$ inch (1.6 mm) from the edge to bring the needle to the top side.

7. Stitch over to the next edge bead, bringing the needle through the backings approximately $^1/_{16}$ inch (1.6 mm) from the edge to the back side (figure 13).

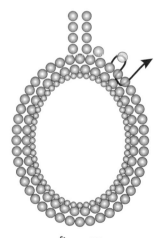

figure 13

8. Repeat steps 3 through 7 until you have circled the cabochon.

9. To add the first twisted strand, stitch up through the first edge bead and the first picot bead. You will

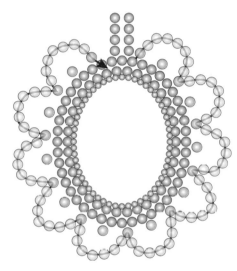

figure 14

10. Add the beads and pass the needle through the third picot bead. In other words, skip the second picot bead and pass through the next, or third, picot bead.

11. Add the beads and continue around the cabochon, skipping every other picot bead and passing through the next picot bead. End by stitching down through the edge bead.

12. Stitch over to the empty picot bead near where you started the previous strand. Stitch up through the edge bead and through the picot bead.

13. Pick up the added beads. Start under the previous strand and loop over it to pass through the next empty picot bead (figure 15).

14. Repeat step 13 around the cabochon until done.

15. Stitch down through the next edge bead and to the back side. Tie a knot, weave in the ends, and cut.

16. Add needles to the tail threads, stitch the ends down into the fabric and tie knots, then weave in the ends and cut the threads.

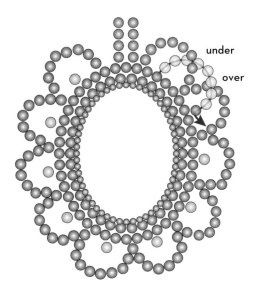

under

over

figure 15

Cabochon: **Glass**
Bezel: **Picot**
Edge: **Twisted**
Attachment: **Top loop**

Cabochon: **Adventurine donuts with tiger-eye**
Bezel: **Standard**
Edge: **Twisted**
Attachment: **Top loop**

Cabochon: **Moon agate**
Bezel: **Standard**
Edge: **Twisted**
Attachment: **Top bail ladder**

Variations: Add a bead between the edge bead and the picot bead to lift the twist out away from the cabochon as shown in the necklace on the left. You can also add beads into the twist strand for interest, as in the cabochon on the right. Try using different colors of beads for the twist strands for another interesting design look. Or use the twisted edge to surround multiple cabochons, as in the middle necklace.

Cabochon: **Dyed howlite**
Bezel: **Standard**
Edge: **Star edge using brick stitch**
Attachment: **Top bail ladder**

Cabochon: **Mustard jasper**
Bezel: **Standard**
Edge: **Star edge using brick stitch**
Attachment: **Top bail ladder**

Cabochon: **Florite**
Bezel: **Standard**
Edge: **Star edge using brick stitch**
Attachment: **Top bail ladder**

Star Edge Using Brick Stitch

The basic edge provides a perfect foundation for expanding the design using a brick stitch (also known as a Cheyenne stitch). The outside of the basic edge has the same bead-and-thread pattern as if it were done using a brick stitch, so adding designs using that stitch are relatively easy. You can add more rows or create a design like the examples above. (The illustrations below show this edge stitch with a top bail ladder stitch attachment; see chapter four.)

INSTRUCTIONS

1. Thread a needle with approximately 2 yards (1.83 m) of beading thread (this technique is worked single-thread).

2. Insert the needle through the backings from the back side, approximately $^1/_{16}$ inch (1.6 mm) from the edge, leaving a tail approximately 9 inches (22.9 cm) long.

3. Stitch up through the first edge bead.

4. Pick up two beads.

5. Stitch around the thread loop two beads over to the right, and stitch back up through the second added bead (figure 16).

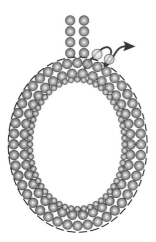

figure 16

6. Pick up one bead.

7. Stitch the thread around the next loop, and stitch back up through the added bead (figure 17).

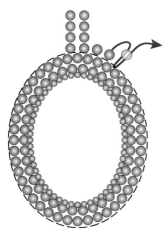

figure 17

8. Repeat steps 6 and 7 so that there is a total of four beads added on top of the basic edge.

9. Pick up two beads.

10. Stitch the thread around the loop two beads over to the left, and stitch back up through the second added bead (figure 18).

figure 18

11. Repeat steps 6 and 7 so that there is a total of three beads on top of the four-bead row.

12. Create the next two-bead row using steps 9 and 10 and going the the other direction (figure 19).

figure 19

13. The final row is one bead wide. Pick up one bead and stitch down through the next bead underneath, changing direction. Stitch across and up through the beads again (figure 20).

figure 20

14. Now stitch down through all the added rows to the edge beads. Use a running stitch (see the side-bar) to move your needle to the next empty edge bead to start the next point.

15. Repeat all the steps for each star point.

16. To finish, stitch down to the backings, tie a knot, weave the ends in, and cut the thread.

Variations: You can change the size of the star points or mix them in with pointed-edge stitches for a variety of designs.

Running Stitch

Although edge-beading stitches are the focus of this chapter, I need to introduce you to a different kind of stitch called the *running stitch*. This stitch is used throughout cabochon beadwork to "travel" from one place to another around the cabochon. In other words, in many cases your needle will be in one spot but your design calls for the needle to be in another spot (say, four beads over) in order to continue with your beading. This is the stitch to use to get to that spot.

The running stitch is done simply by stitching up and down through the backings (from the top side to the back side to the top side to the back side, etc.), making each stitch approximately ¹⁄₁₆ inch (1.6 mm) long. The position to place the stitches is between the edge row and the base row (or the last additional row if your design included that option), as shown in the illustration.

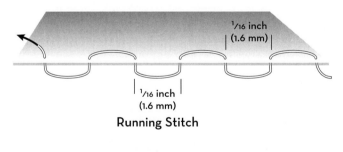

Running Stitch

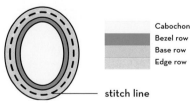

Cabochon
Bezel row
Base row
Edge row

stitch line

Cabochon: **Botswana agate**
Bezel: **Bead-raised**
Edge: **Ruffled using brick stitch**
Attachment: **Back side bead**

Cabochon: **Dichroic glass**
Bezel: **Window**
Edge: **Ruffled using brick stitch**
Attachment: **Top bail ladder**

Cabochon: **Mustard jasper**
Bezel: **Standard**
Edge: **Ruffled using brick stitch**
Attachment: **Back side bead**

Ruffled Edge Using Brick Stitch

You can also create a ruffle using the brick stitch. In the instructions below, the first two rows are doubled up every third space; in other words, as you add a bead and stitch around each loop of thread between edge beads, you stitch twice—adding a total of two beads—around every third loop. The subsequent rows are normal brick stitch. When creating a necklace with a ruffled-edge cabochon, use the back side bead method (see chapter four) to attach the necklace so that the design of the ruffle is not interrupted.

INSTRUCTIONS

1. Thread a needle with approximately 2 yards (1.83 m) of beading thread (this technique is worked single-thread).

2. Insert the needle through the backings from the back side, approximately ¹⁄₁₆ inch (1.6 mm) from the edge, leaving a tail of beading thread approximately 9 inches (22.9 cm) long.

3. Stitch up through any edge bead.

4. To start the first row, pick up two beads.

5. Stitch the thread around the loop two beads over, and stitch back up through the second added bead (figure 21).

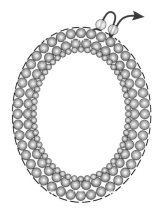

figure 21

6. Pick up one bead.

7. Stitch around the same thread loop, and stitch back up through the added bead (figure 22).

figure 22

8. Pick up one bead.

9. Stitch around the next thread loop, and stitch back up through the added bead (figure 23).

figure 23

10. Pick up one bead.

11. Stitch around the next thread loop, and stitch back up through the added bead (figure 24).

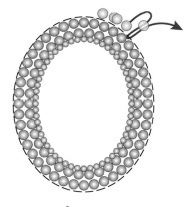

figure 24

12. Pick up one bead.

13. Stitch around the next thread loop, and then stitch back up through the added bead.

14. Repeat steps 6 through 13 until the row is complete.

15. To close off a row, stitch down into the first bead added when the row was started and through the bead under it in the previous row. Then stitch up into the bead next to that bead and back up through the first added bead of the row you've just finished (figure 25). You're now ready to do the next row.

figure 25

16. Stitch the second row the same as the first, doubling up every third section. In other words, repeat steps 4 through 15.

17. For the third and subsequent rows, do standard brick stitch; do not double up. That is, repeat steps 12 and 13 around the entire edge.

18. *Optional:* For the final row, you can use the standard brick stitch as in the instructions above, or use the picot edge variation discussed in chapter two (page 21).

19. To finish the ruffle, stitch through the beads down through the rows to the backing. Tie a knot, weave in the end, and cut the thread.

20. Add a needle on the tail thread. Tie a knot, weave in the end, and cut the thread.

Variations: In the instructions above, beads are doubled up every third stitch—two standard brick stitches, then two beads stitched into the third. You can make a smoother, less pronounced ruffle by doubling up every fourth stitch, or make it fuller by doubling up every second stitch.

Cabochon: **Rhodochrosite**
Bezel: **Bead-raised**
Edge: **Scalloped**
Attachment: **Lifted turn bead**

Cabochon: **Crackle glass**
Bezel: **Bead-raised**
Edge: **Scalloped**
Attachment: **Direct**

Cabochon: **White adventurine**
Bezel: **Standard**
Edge: **Scalloped**

Scalloped Edge

This edge incorporates a series of accent center beads into the edge to create a beautiful scalloped design. The method has a repeating pattern and therefore requires a count on the edge beads that is divisible by the number of beads in the repeating pattern. An alternative is to work the pattern simultaneously from each side to meet at the center of the bottom. If the beads are an even count of the pattern, you can simply join them at the meeting point. If the beads are not an even count, you can create a variation of the pattern at the bottom so that your design is still symmetrical. (The illustrations below show this edge stitch with a top bail ladder stitch attachment; see chapter four.)

INSTRUCTIONS

1. Select the accent beads that you want to use for the scalloped edge in your design.

2. Before you start actually beading the edge, you need to determine how to space the scallops, which depends on the size and shapes of the beads you've chosen. Use a needle to attach a center bead temporarily to any bead in the basic edge (figure 26).

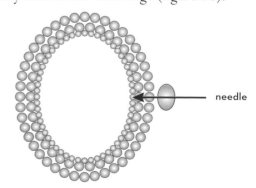

needle

figure 26

Count the number of edge beads from the middle of the center bead to the outside edge on the right of the center bead and insert a needle in that outermost edge bead. Use the same count from the center bead out to the left and insert another needle in that bead (figure 27).

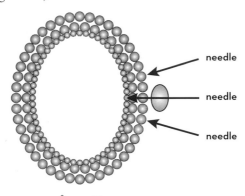

figure 27

The center bead needs to be able to rest between the two added needles, with a gap between the center bead and the needle on each side of at least one-half the width of a single seed bead. Move the side needles as necessary to produce that gap on each side (figure 28).

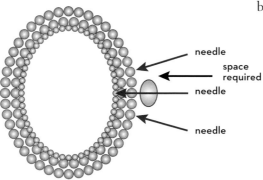

figure 28

Now count the number of edge beads in the section, including the beads with the outside needles. (The count should always come out to an odd number, because there should be an equal number of edge beads on both sides of the center bead's middle, plus the one directly below it.) Remove all

the needles. Calculate the number of scallops and their spacing based on the count you just determined and the total number of edge beads around the cabochon.

3. Now you're ready to start beading. Thread a needle with approximately 3 yards (2.74 m) of beading thread; this method is worked double-thread, so move the needle to the center to produce a double strand.

4. At the point where the first center bead will be attached, insert the needle through the backings from the back side to the top side, approximately $\frac{1}{16}$ inch (1.6 mm) from the edge, leaving a tail approximately 9 inches (22.9 cm) long.

5. Stitch up through the edge bead.

6. Pick up a center bead and a seed bead.

7. Stitch back down through the center bead and edge bead to the back side (figure 29). Hold the seed bead with one hand and pull the thread with the other hand to adjust the tension so the center bead sits firmly on the edge bead.

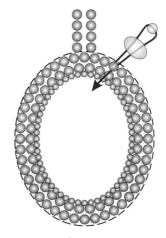

figure 29

8. Stitch up through the backings to the top side approximately $\frac{1}{16}$ inch (1.6 mm) from the edge.

9. Using a running stitch (see sidebar on page 37), cross over to the edge bead that will be first in the scalloped section, based on the count you determined in step 2. Then stitch down through the backings to the back side.

10. Stitch up through the first edge bead in the section.

11. Pick up the number of beads needed to create the first half of the scallop loop (this will depend on your design and the beads themselves), and go through the seed bead added to the center bead. Pick up the beads needed for the final half of the scallop loop. You should be using the same number of beads for the first and second halves of the loop.

12. Stitch down through the last edge bead in the section to the back side (figure 30).

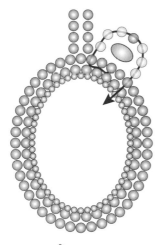

figure 30

13. Stitch up through the backing to the top side approximately ¹⁄₁₆ inch (1.6 mm) from the edge of the backing.

14. Now, using a running stitch, "travel" over to the center of the next section; then stitch down through the backings to the back side to start another scallop (figure 31).

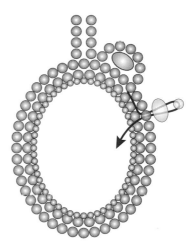

figure 31

15. Repeat steps 5 through 13 for each scallop.

16. To finish the edge, stitch through the backings to the back side. Tie a knot, weave in the end, and cut the thread. Add a needle to the tail thread. Tie a knot, weave in the end, and cut.

Variation: One variation you may want to try is simply to pick up the accent bead within the loop (figure 32).

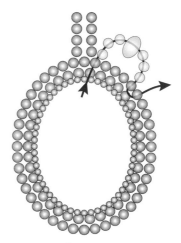

figure 32

Cabochon: **Agate**
Bezel: **Small cabochon variation**
Edge: **Pointed with fringe**
Attachment: **Direct**

Cabochon: **Fossilized coral**
Bezel: **Standard**
Edge: **Fringe, branch fringe**
Attachment: **Top loop**

Cabochon: **Vintage glass**
Bezel: **Bead-raised**
Edge: **Pointed with fringe**
Attachment: **Top loop**

Fringes

There's nothing like subtly swaying fringe for adding movement and interest to a piece. Basic beaded cabochons are perfect for all kinds of beaded fringe styles, and fringes are one of the easiest edge techniques to do. You can add fringes to the bottom portion only and then use another edge technique on the sides and top (it's important to add the fringe first so that you can position it properly in your design). Or use fringes all the way around the edge (adding very short fringes for the sides and top) for a fanciful, fun design. The instructions below are for standard straight fringe applied only on the bottom portion of the cabochon. The length and number of fringe strands, and the size and number of beads in each one, is up to you. In most cases, however,

straight fringe ends with a larger bead for weight, and then a small *turn bead*. You can also use other beadwork fringe techniques, such as branch or twisted (refer to any good general beading book for details on those methods). Regardless of the fringe design or technique you choose, the method for attaching fringe to your cabochon's edge and backings, described here and shown in figure 33, will be the same.

turn bead

figure 33

INSTRUCTIONS

1. Cut approximately 6 yards (5.49 m) of thread, and thread a needle on each end. You'll use half the thread to add fringe on the right side and the other half to add fringe on the left side.

2. At the middle of the bottom of the cabochon, insert one needle through the backings from the back side to the top side, approximately $\frac{1}{16}$ inch (1.6 mm) from the backings' edge. Pull the thread so that 3 yards (2.74 m) are on each side (front and back) of the cabochon.

3. Using the thread and needle on the back side of the cabochon, stitch down through the center edge bead.

4. Pick up beads for the fringe according to your design, ending with a turn bead.

5. Stitch back up through the fringe beads (except for the turn bead).

6. Stitch up through the edge bead, staying on the back side.

7. Stitch up through the backings to the top side approximately $\frac{1}{16}$ inch (1.6 mm) from the edge of the backings.

8. Stitch over to the next edge bead and down into the backings to the back side approximately $\frac{1}{16}$ inch (1.6 mm) from the edge.

9. Pass the needle through the edge bead.

10. Repeat steps 4 through 9 until all fringes on the side are done.

11. Tie a knot, weave in the end, and cut the thread.

12. Pick up the other needle and thread.

13. Stitch over to the next edge bead down through the backings from the top side to the back side approximately $\frac{1}{16}$ inch (1.6 mm) from the edge.

14. Pass the needle through the edge bead.

15. Repeat steps 4 through 9 until all fringes on the side are done.

16. Tie a knot, weave in the end, and cut the thread.

CHAPTER 4

Cabochon: **Fossilized coral**
Bezel: **Standard**
Edge: **Fringed**
Attachment: **Top loop**

Cabochon: **Botswana agate,**
           gray onyx
Bezel: **Bead-raised, standard**
Edge: **Points with tassel**
Attachment: **Turn bead**

Cabochon: **Goldstone**
Bezel: **Standard**
Edge: **Joined points variation**
Attachment: **Direct**

attachment methods

In this chapter, we'll look at different ways to attach beading to a basic beaded cabochon to create a necklace, bracelet, or other project. Sometimes, choosing a method of attachment for a particular piece is purely a matter of design preference. In other cases, there are practical issues that dictate using one method over another. For example, if the necklace section will be a string of large, chunky beads, it would be inappropriate to use the direct attachment method (the first approach described in this chapter), because the cabochon would be lifted out from the body by the beads and would not lie properly.

There are many other factors to keep in mind, too. For instance, large or heavy cabochons need to be attached using a method that will easily hold the weight. At the same time, even though a particular method may hold the weight, your design will be more visually appealing if the method also has a bold, sturdy appearance. Likewise, small, delicate cabochons need to be balanced with delicate designs and attachment methods. All of the instructions that follow assume that you've already given your design some thought and chosen the beads that you'll string to create the project.

Cabochon: **Crazy lace agate**
Bezel: **Bead-raised**
Edge: **Raw**
Attachment: **Direct**

Cabochon: **Dichroic glass**
Bezel: **Standard**
Edge: **Pointed with tassel**
Attachment: **Direct**

Cabochon: **Dichroic glass**
Bezel: **Window**
Edge: **Pointed with fringe**
Attachment: **Direct**

Direct Attachment Method

This method is very easy to do and is attractive and useful in most designs. You simply string the necklace (or bracelet, etc.) beads directly into the cabochon edge beads. Each side is worked separately. You can position where you put the entry point on the edge to accommodate your design. For example, the entry points for a choker could be on the sides of the cabochon. Short necklaces should have an entry point that's wider from the center of the top (as in the necklace above left), while long necklaces may have a deep V-shape and enter very near the top center (as in the necklace above center).

INSTRUCTIONS

1. Thread a needle with approximately 3 yards (2.74 m) of beading thread; this method is worked double-thread, so move the needle to the center to produce a double strand.

2. Start from the end where the finding will be attached. Use a size 5° or 6° seed bead and loop the thread around it with a tail approximately 6 inches (15.2 cm) long (figure 1). This is referred to as a *stop bead* because it stops the other beads from falling off the thread as you work.

tail

figure 1

3. String your beads for the necklace or bracelet, designing from the back and going toward the cabochon in the center.

4. Once you have all the beads for the strand on, stitch the needle directly into the selected edge bead, keeping the needle to the top side.

5. Now stitch down through the backings, approximately $\frac{1}{16}$ inch (1.6 mm) from the outside edge of the backings, pulling the needle through to the back side.

6. Stitch back up through the edge bead from the back side, and continue through all the beads in the strand to the stop bead (figure 2).

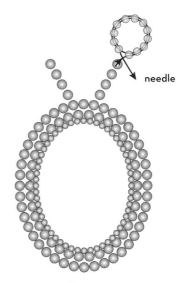

figure 3

figure 2

7. Remove the loop from the stop bead and pass the needle through the bead.

8. Pick up 15 size 11° or 12° seed beads.

9. Go through the beads again to create a loop (figure 3).

10. Adjust the position of the beads to get the proper tension.

11. Use the needle end and the tail thread to tie a square knot.

12. Put a needle on the tail thread and stitch 2 or 3 inches (5.1 or 7.6 cm) down into the bead strand portion.

13. Take the original needle and go through the bead loop again.

14. Take the original needle and stitch 2 or 3 inches (5.1 or 7.6 cm) down into the bead strand portion.

15. Pull on the threads to move the knot into the bead that was the stop bead.

16. Trim all the ends close to the beads in the strand.

17. Use two jump rings on each side to attach the findings.

Variations: You can use the direct attachment method to join several basic beaded cabochons to each other. Then add beads in between the cabochons to enhance your design. This method is also perfect for multistrand designs; attach each strand directly to the cabochon's edge.

Cabochon: Crazy lace agate
Bezel: Standard
Edge: Raw
Attachment: Direct

Cabochon: Jade
Bezel: Standard
Edge: Pointed with drop
Attachment: Direct

Cabochon: Indian agate
Bezel: Bead-raised
Edge: Raw
Attachment: Direct

Cabochon: **Rhyolite**
Bezel: **Bead-raised**
Edge: **Raw**
Attachment: **Turn bead**

Cabochon: **Carnelian agate, mustard jasper**
Bezel: **Standard**
Edge: **Pointed**
Attachment: **Turn bead**

Cabochon: **Fluorite**
Bezel: **Bead-raised**
Edge: **Pointed**
Attachment: **Turn bead**

Turn Bead Method

This technique creates a clean, simple attachment. It's easy to do and, by changing the bead sizes used, can produce a variety of looks.

Cabochon with turn bead attachment

INSTRUCTIONS

1. Thread a needle with approximately 2 yards (1.83 m) of beading thread (this technique is worked single-thread).

2. Select two or more beads to sew onto the beaded cabochon edge. You'll be stitching through these beads several times, and the necklace threads will also go through these beads, so make sure the beads have holes large enough to accommodate all of the threads.

3. Determine the position of the added beads at the center of the cabochon edge beads.

4. From the back side of the beaded cabochon, stitch up through the backings to the top side, approximately $1/16$ inch (1.6 mm) from the edge.

Be careful not to pierce any of the threads already there. Now stitch up through the edge bead that will be to the outside edge of one of the added beads (figure 4). Leave a tail approximately 9 inches (22.9 cm) long.

figure 4

5. String all the added beads onto the thread.

6. Stitch down through the edge bead that is on the outside edge on the other side of the added beads. Stay on the top side of the beaded cabochon.

7. Stitch down through the backings to the back side approximately $\frac{1}{16}$ inch (1.6 mm) from the edge, and then stitch up through the same edge bead.

8. Use your fingers to nudge the beads into place so that the holes for the added beads line up parallel with the outside edge of the beaded cabochon. Throughout this process, keep nudging the beads into place.

9. Pass the needle through the nearest added bead, then stitch down through the nearest hole in an edge bead, staying to the top side. Stitch down through the backings approximately $\frac{1}{16}$ inch (1.6 mm) from the edge, and then stitch up through the same edge bead (figure 5).

figure 5

10. Repeat step 9 until you are at the end of the added beads.

11. Stitch though all the added beads to the other side.

12. Repeat the entire process from step 6 through step 10.

13. Finally, stitch to the back side. Tie a square knot in the tail thread. Weave the ends into the backings and cut.

14. To attach the necklace, simply string the cabochon through the holes in the added beads while you're stringing the necklace (figure 6).

figure 6

Variations: You can create different designs with the turn bead method by changing the number of beads used for the turn beads. In the photo on the left below, the entire width of the cabochon was done with turn beads. In the middle is an example of an extended length. The example on the right uses a 4 mm bead in the turn beads. The 4 mm bead is also used on the edge décor, giving the design a more fluid appearance.

Cabochon: Montana agate
Bezel: Bead-raised
Edge: Fringe
Attachment: Turn bead

Cabochon: Septarian jasper
Bezel: Bead-raised
Edge: Pointed
Attachment: Turn bead

Cabochon: Pyrite chunk
Bezel: Window
Edge: Scallops, fringe, points
Attachment: Turn bead

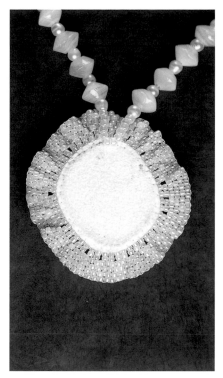

Cabochon: **Botswana agate**
Bezel: **Bead-raised**
Edge: **Ruffled using brick stitch**
Attachment: **Back side bead**

Back side attachment of cabochon
on left

Back side attachment of cabochon
on right

Cabochon: **Eagle-eye agate**
Bezel: **Bead-raised**
Edge: **Fringe**
Attachment: **Back side bead**

Back Side Bead Method

This method is useful for creations with an edge design that you want to continue all the way around the cabochon without interruption by a necklace attachment. The technique calls for sewing some beads onto the back side of the beaded cabochon. The pendant is then strung onto the necklace through the holes in those beads. The beaded cabochon is lifted out from the body by the beads in the back. Accordingly, this method is especially appropriate when the edge creates some depth, such as with ruffled or branch fringe edges.

INSTRUCTIONS

1. Thread a needle with approximately 1 yard (.9 m) of beading thread (this technique is worked single-thread).

2. Select two or more beads to sew onto the back of the beaded cabochon. You'll be stitching through these beads several times, and the necklace threads will also go through these beads, so make sure the beads have holes that are large enough to accommodate all of the threads. However, since this adds depth onto the back, select small beads so that the beads are as close to the backing as possible. Usually, size 8° or 9° seed beads work well.

3. Determine the position of the added beads on the back side of the beaded cabochon. The position needs to be in from the top edge of the outer backing toward the center, but close enough to the edge to allow the needle to go through the backings without running into the cabochon.

4. From the back side, at the point where you want to place the first added bead, stitch the needle through the backings to the top side. Leave a tail approximately 9 inches (22.9 cm) long.

5. Without interfering with the beadwork on the top side of the beaded cabochon, stitch over and bring the needle back down through the backings to the back side at the point where you want the last added bead.

6. Add the beads onto the needle; thread and stitch them down into place, bringing the needle to the top side.

7. Sew each of the added beads onto the back side, stitching through the backings from the top side to the back side (figure 7). When stitching on the top side, be careful that you do not interfere with the beadwork there.

figure 7

8. Finally, bring the needle and thread to the back side near the tail. Tie a square knot in the thread ends. Weave the ends into the backing and cut them.

9. To attach the cabochon, simply string the pendant through the holes in the added beads while you're stringing the necklace. In your design, use size 8° or 9° seed beads for the part of the necklace strand that's behind the cabochon so it'll lie properly.

Cabochon: **Mexican lace agate**
Bezel: **Standard**
Edge: **Raw**
Attachment: **Top bail ladder**

Cabochon: **Mahogany obsidian**
Bezel: **Standard**
Edge: **Points and fringe**
Attachment: **Top bail ladder**

Cabochon: **Mustard jasper**
Bezel: **Standard**
Edge: **Pointed**
Attachment: **Top bail ladder**

Top Bail Ladder Stitch Method

Necklaces that are constructed with large, chunky beads in the strand require special consideration in the way the necklace is attached. The top bail ladder stitch method is particularly appropriate for those designs because the strip, or bail, that it creates provides a hinge-like mechanism that ensures that both the beads in the necklace and the pendant will lie properly against the body.

The strip is created with a two-needle ladder stitch. The instructions below are for a three-bead-wide strip, but you can use them to make the bail almost any width. When the instructions call for three beads, just substitute the number of beads in the width you want for your design.

INSTRUCTIONS

1. Cut two lengths of beading thread, each approximately 2 ½ yards (2.29 m) long. Thread each length onto its own needle; this method is worked double-thread, so move the needles to the centers to produce double strands.

2. With one of the two needles, stitch up from the back side through the backings to the top side. Insert the needle below the edge bead that is under the spacing for the bead row to be added. Leave a tail approximately 9 inches (22.9 cm) long. Stitch up through the edge bead (blue, figure 8).

3. Repeat step 2 with the other thread on the other side (red, figure 8).

4. Add three beads onto the first needle (blue, figure 8). Position the beads to lie on top of the beads in the previous row.

5. Take the other needle and stitch through the three beads just added (red, figure 8). Take the two ends and pull and adjust the bead positions (figure 9).

figure 8

figure 9

6. Repeat steps 4 and 5 until you have the desired length for the bail. It is wise to test that the bail will fit over the beads you intend to use for your necklace before you finish the bail.

7. To complete the loop for the bail, take one of the needles and stitch through the beads in the second added row. Repeat on the other side with the other needle. Pull on the threads to create the bail loop. Then, using one needle, stitch down to the first row, but only to the middle bead, not all the way through the row. From the front side, stitch down into the edge bead. Stitch into the backings to bring the needle to the back side (figure 10). Repeat on the other side.

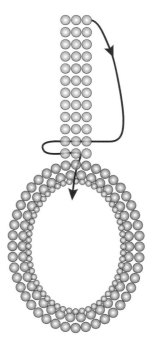

figure 10

8. On the back side, tie a square knot with the thread in the two needles. Weave the ends into the backing and cut the threads. Thread needles onto the tail ends, tie a square knot on each side, weave in the ends, and cut.

9. To add a necklace, string the strand as usual. If the bail is large enough to fit over all the beads, you can simply slip the pendant on after you've finished stringing. If not, you'll need to put the pendant in the center as you're stringing the necklace.

Variation: This method can easily be adapted to create a beaded cabochon ring. Simply create the strip as long as needed for the ring size. Instead of looping the strip around to create a bail, attach the end of the strip to the other side of the cabochon to create the ring.

Cabochon: **Brecciated jasper**
Bezel: **Standard**
Edge: **Fringe**
Attachment: **Top loop**

Cabochon: **White aventurine**
Bezel: **Picot**
Edge: **Fringe**
Attachment: **Top loop**

Cabochon: **Handblown glass**
Bezel: **Bead-raised**
Edge: **Fringe**
Attachment: **Top loop**

Top Loop Method

This method not only provides a useful way to attach a necklace, but it also adds a wonderful design element. The pendant is floated on the necklace so that it can slide across the necklace, allowing more freedom of movement than other methods. Necklace-beading techniques such as tubular peyote are especially attractive in combination with this particular attachment.

The instructions are for a six-bead-wide loop, three on each side. These instructions also assume that the center is between two beads on the top. The number of loops to use is a design decision and can be two or more; just alter the instructions below as needed to create the number of loops you want for your project.

INSTRUCTIONS

1. Thread a needle with approximately 3 yards (2.74 m) of beading thread; this method is worked double-thread, so move the needle to the center to produce a double strand.

2. From the back side, stitch up through the backings, leaving a tail approximately 9 inches (22.9 cm) long. The needle should enter approximately $\frac{1}{16}$ inch (1.6 mm) from the edge, below the right-center edge bead. Stitch up through the right-center edge bead. Pick up 20 beads and stitch down through the edge bead that is the fourth bead from the center, staying on the top side. Stitch down through the backings to the back side approximately $\frac{1}{16}$ inch (1.6 mm) from the edge. Then stitch across to the fifth bead from the center to bring the needle to the top side, entering approximately $\frac{1}{16}$ inch (1.6 mm) from the edge. Stitch up through the fifth bead (figure 11).

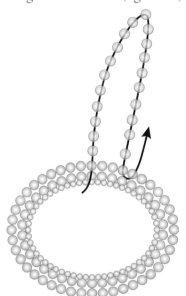

figure 11

3. Pick up 21 beads and stitch down through the edge bead that is second from the center, staying on the top side. Be careful to position the loop so that it is outside and in front of the previous loop. Stitch down through the backings to the back side approximately $\frac{1}{16}$ inch (1.6 mm) from the edge. (It's helpful at this stage to put a pencil through the loops as a substitute for the necklace beads. This will help you keep the loops positioned correctly.) Stitch across to the third

bead from the center to bring the needle to the top side, entering approximately $\frac{1}{16}$ inch (1.6 mm) from the edge. Stitch up through the third bead (figure 12).

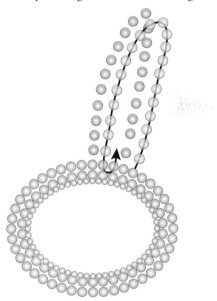

figure 12

4. Pick up 22 beads and stitch down through the edge bead that is sixth from the center, staying on the top side. Remember to be careful to position each loop so that it is outside and in front of the previous loop. Stitch down through the backings to the back side approximately $\frac{1}{16}$ inch (1.6 mm) from the edge (figure 13).

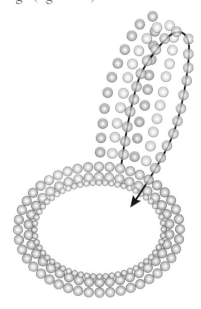

figure 13

5. Stitch back up through the same edge bead.

6. Stitch back through all the added beads, retracing all the stitches to reinforce the loops. Continue until you go through all three loops and return to the center.

7. Repeat steps 1 through 6 on the other side of the cabochon.

8. Finally, bring the needle through to the back side near the tail thread. Tie the ends with a square knot; weave them into the backings, and cut.

Note: In the instructions above, the center of the cabochon is between two beads. If the center point falls at a bead rather than between two beads, you can still use this method by allowing the first loops on each side to share five beads (figure 14).

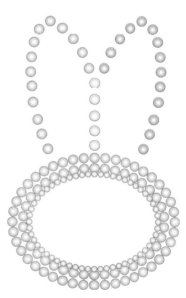

figure 14

Variations: You can vary this design to create different effects by changing the number of loops or the number of beads in the loop (which makes loops longer or shorter). You can also vary the number of beads in adjacent loops. For example, you might make the first loop 18 beads, the second loop 21 beads, and the third loop 24 beads. This will create a deeper V-shape profile for the loops.

Another way to vary this attachment is to position the loops to the inside and in back of the previous loops instead of outside and in front (as shown in the photo on the left).

Cabochon: **Montana agate**
Bezel: **Bead-raised**
Edge: **Fringe**
Attachment: **Top loop**

Cabochon: **Brecciated jasper**
Bezel: **Standard**
Edge: **Fringe**
Attachment: **Top loop**

other bezel stitches

This chapter illustrates additional methods for creating a bezel row on a beaded cabochon. Although the bezel technique used for the basic beaded cabochon works for most cabochons, other stitches can be used too, either as decorative features or to solve problems resulting from an unusual slope on the cabochon.

Cabochon: **Dichroic glass**
Bezel: **Bead-raised**
Edge: **Pointed with fringe**
Attachment: **Direct**

Cabochon: **Eagle-eye agate**
Bezel: **Bead-raised**
Edge: **Pointed**
Attachment: **Turn bead**

Cabochon: **Blue lace agate tumbled stone**
Bezel: **Bead-raised**
Edge: **Pointed**
Attachment: **Turn bead**

Bead-Raised Bezel

Cabochons having a thick edge present a unique problem. In order for the bezel row to hold the cabochon in place effectively, the bezel row must be positioned up into the slope of the cabochon.

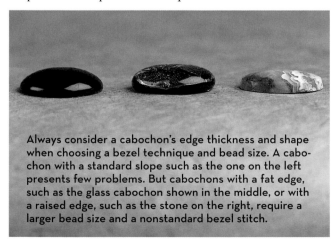

Always consider a cabochon's edge thickness and shape when choosing a bezel technique and bead size. A cabochon with a standard slope such as the one on the left presents few problems. But cabochons with a fat edge, such as the glass cabochon shown in the middle, or with a raised edge, such as the stone on the right, require a larger bead size and a nonstandard bezel stitch.

Some cabochons, however, are cut with an edge that is not evenly sloped. This is particularly true for most glass cabochons, due to the nature of glass when it melts. Many stone cabochons also have cuts that present the same problem.

The simplest solution for this is to use large beads—larger than a size 10° seed bead—on the base row, the row that's applied first. This provides a foundation for the bezel row to rest upon. By using large beads in that outside row, you can easily raise the bezel row. A size 5° or 6° "E" bead will work for most glass cabochons. Thicker edges may require a 4 mm or even a 6 mm bead. The bead size to use depends on the thickness of the edge and your design preferences.

Of course, using larger beads around the cabochon can present its own set of problems. Because the bead is larger, it can be difficult to get a smooth, tight fit around the cabochon. If you use size 5° or 6° seed beads, you can use the standard instructions in chapter two; at that size (and smaller), seed beads aren't uniform—some are thinner and some are thicker—and the variations allow you to get a good fit around the cabochon. However, if you use a larger bead or a bead that is uniform in shape, such as a 4 mm round, you may not be able to get a good fit around the cabochon with the standard four-six backstitch.

You can solve the problem by using a different stitch to apply the beads so that you can manipulate the fit around the cabochon more easily. This stitch is called the *couch stitch*. Essentially, you string the entire row of beads around the cabochon first, and then sew it down into the backing. This allows you to add or subtract beads as needed to obtain a balanced, even spacing. After you've sewn down the row, you stitch on the bezel row.

INSTRUCTIONS
1. Thread a needle with approximately 2 yards (1.83 m) of beading thread (this technique is worked single-thread).

2. Insert the needle up from the back side of the under backing with the needle next to the edge of the cabochon at the top center, or 12 o'clock position. Leave a tail approximately 9 inches (22.9 cm) long.

3. String on the beads for the base row. Add as many beads as necessary to circle the cabochon completely and create a loop by stitching through the first added bead a second time. The beads should fit next to the cabochon edge without a gap. If you have a gap, undo the loop, remove or add a bead or beads as necessary, and try again. You can push the beads around the strand so that they evenly surround the cabochon. This can be a loose fit as long as there are no big gaps between the beads in the strand.

4. Once you've determined the correct number of beads in the strand, stitch through the entire strand again so there are at least two threads in the entire loop (figure 1). If you're using beads as large as 6 mm or more, stitch though the loop again. End by stitching down through the under backing to the back side. Tie a knot.

figure 1

5. In this step, you'll put anchoring stitches at intervals in the row so that the proper spacing is maintained. The stitches will be at three, six, nine, and 12 o'clock (figure 2). You've already done the stitching needed at 12 o'clock. Use your fingers to move the beads around to the proper spacing. Stitch one couch stitch at six o'clock, directly opposite from where you stitched down through the under backing. To do this, bring the needle up through the backing to the top side at the six o'clock position with the needle next to the edge of the cabochon, between the cabochon and the bead row and between two beads. Now stitch down into the under backing, looping over the thread between the beads. The needle should enter near the edge of the cabochon. Pull the thread so that the loop rests on top of the thread between the beads. Don't pull it so tight that the thread between the beads is pulled down toward the backing, but do pull it tight enough that the loop rests on that thread and cannot be seen between the beads.

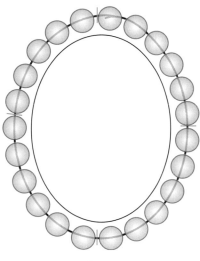

figure 2

6. Repeat step 5 to stitch at both the three o'clock and the nine o'clock positions. Make sure you move the beads as necessary to place the stitches in the correct positions.

7. Now, with the bead row secured into quarters, stitch down between each of the beads, working around the cabochon, starting where you stitched last (figure 3). Move the beads within the quarter as needed to provide an even spacing. Remember, the needle should be stitched up next to the edge of the cabochon, looped over the thread between the beads, and down into the backing next to the cabochon. And again, it's important to tighten the thread so that the loop rests on top of the thread and is not visible between the beads, but it shouldn't be so tight that the thread between the beads is pulled down toward the backing.

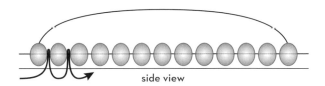

side view

figure 3

8. Stitch completely around the cabochon, and then stitch to the back side. Tie a knot, weave in the end, and cut the thread. Then thread a needle on the tail thread, tie a knot, weave in the end, and cut.

9. Stitch on the bezel row according to the instructions in chapter two, or use one of the other bezel stitches described in this chapter. Because the first bead row is made of larger beads and therefore raised, you'll need to take particular care not to pull threads down too tightly while you're attaching the bezel row. The bezel row should rest on top of the base row beads and should not be pulled down so much that it creates a separation between the cabochon edge and the base row beads.

Cabochon: **Carnelian agate, black onyx**
Bezel: **Window, standard**
Edge: **Turned bead**
Attachment: **Direct**

Cabochon: **Botswana agate**
Bezel: **Window**
Edge: **Pointed**
Attachment: **Top bail ladder**

Cabochon: **Agate**
Bezel: **Window**
Edge: **Fringe**
Attachment: **Direct**

Window Bezel

This method creates an elevated bezel with "windows" between the base row and the bezel row. It allows you to place the bezel row deep toward the center of the cabochon while still keeping much of the stone visible. Essentially, you create small fringes that stand up from the row of beads around the cabochon (the base row), and then join them together using turn beads at the ends of the fringe. You can create a variety of designs by changing the length of the fringe strands, the sizes and colors of the beads used, and the spacing of the fringe strands around the cabochon.

There are two methods that can be used to determine the spacing of the windows. One method is to use the bead count on the base row already applied around the cabochon. You can count those beads and use a number that divides evenly into it to space the fringes. A spacing of every four beads works well.

Because you created the base row using a four-six backstitch, most of the row works out to a four-bead count. You can adjust this as necessary by remembering the number of beads used to close the loop (see page 18) and also remembering to adjust for the two beads you added to start the row. If you closed with two beads, you don't need to count the row; it will work every four beads. If you closed by a different count, simply adjust one or more of the windows to make up the difference.

The other method that can be used to space the fringes is simply to measure and mark whatever distances you desire. Just use a pencil or pen to mark the under backing near the bead row with a small dot at each place where you want a fringe. You can space the positions evenly or create an uneven design.

The instructions below create a window that's one bead tall and spaced every three beads of the base row. Note that the instructions say to stitch through the holes in the bead row previously applied. If the holes in that bead row are already filled so that it is too difficult to pass a needle and thread through them, simply stitch down into the under backing instead.

Instructions

1. Thread a needle with approximately 2 yards (1.83 m) of beading thread (this technique is worked single-thread).

2. Insert the needle through the under backing from the back side and bring it to the top side. The needle should be inserted next to the edge of the cabochon, between the cabochon and the base row of beads. Leave a tail approximately 9 inches (22.9 cm) long. Insert the needle through two beads of the base row.

3. Pick up two beads, then stitch back down through the first of the two added beads, leaving the second bead as the turn bead. Hold the turn bead with one hand and pull on the thread with the other to adjust the tension. The fringe should sit comfortably on the previous bead row. Do not pull so tight that the fringe flares out. Stitch through the next three beads on the base row, repeat step 3 around the entire cabochon (figure 4).

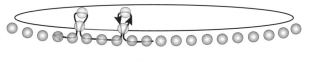

figure 4

4. Stitch down through the backing to the back side.

5. Bring the needle to the top side by stitching over to the nearest small fringe. Stitch up through the fringe beads, including the end turn bead.

6. Determine the number of beads to add between the fringes. Make sure the fringes are lying straight,

and test the number of beads you'll need to span the spaces between them.

7. Pick up the number of beads determined in step 6. Sometimes, you may need to adjust this number between any two particular fringe points by adding or leaving off one bead. Make these adjustments as needed so that the fringes lie straight and the bezel row is lying properly on the cabochon. Stitch through the next fringe (figure 5).

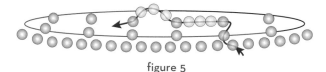

figure 5

8. Repeat step 7 around the cabochon (figure 6).

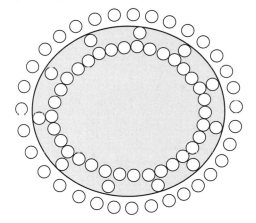

figure 6

9. Once all the beads have been added, continue stitching through the beads in this row. Stitch around and around until the holes of the beads are filled with thread. This will strengthen the row and make the beads line up properly next to each other.

10. End near a fringe. Stitch down through the fringe and through the under backing.

11. Tie a knot, weave in the end, and cut the thread. Thread a needle on the tail thread, tie a knot in it, weave in the end, and cut.

Cabochon: **Quartz**
Bezel: **Picot**
Edge: **Fringe**
Attachment: **Top loop**

Cabochon: **Crazy lace agate**
Bezel: **Picot**
Edge: **Pointed**
Attachment: **Top loop**

Cabochon: **Carnelian agate**
Bezel: **Picot**
Edge: **Fringe**
Attachment: **Top loop**

Picot Bezel

Like the window bezel technique, this method also lifts the bezel row of beads toward the center of the cabochon and creates windows that keep most of the stone visible. But it also creates a delicate, lacy look, with tiny prongs of beads holding the row. It's especially useful for adding a decorative flair to the bezel for cabochons that are a solid color, such as black onyx or hematite.

To determine the spacing of the picots, use either of the two methods described in the window-bezel section for spacing windows: Calculate the spacing to divide evenly into the base row's bead count, adjusting as necessary to compensate for any modifications you made when closing that row, or simply measure and mark the spacing you want around the cabochon.

The instructions below use a spacing of every four beads of the bead row previously applied. Note that the instructions say to stitch through the holes in the bead row previously applied. If the holes in that bead row are already filled so that it is too difficult to pass a needle and thread through them, simply stitch down into the under backing instead.

figure 8

INSTRUCTIONS

1. Thread a needle with approximately 1 yard (.91 m) of beading thread (this method is worked single-thread).

2. Insert the needle through the under backing from the back side. The needle should be inserted next to the edge of the cabochon, between the cabochon and the base row of beads. Leave a tail approximately 9 inches (22.9 cm) long. Insert the needle through two beads of the base row.

3. Pick up three beads, and create the picot by stitching back though the last of the two beads in the base row and then four more beads in that row (figure 7).

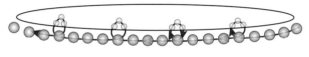

figure 7

4. Repeat step 3 around the entire cabochon.

5. Stitch down through the beads and the backing to the back side.

6. Tie a knot, weave in the end, and cut. Thread a needle on the tail thread. Tie a knot, weave in the end, and cut.

7. Thread a needle with approximately 1½ yards (1.4 m) of beading thread (you'll still be working single-thread).

8. Stitch though the top bead on one of the picots. Pick up one bead, loop the thread around, and stitch though the top picot bead. Pull the thread so that the bead rests on top of the picot and the tail thread is approximately 9 inches (22.9 cm) long. Finally, stitch back up through the added bead (figure 8).

9. Determine the number of beads to add between the picots, plus one to sit on top of the next picot. Make sure the picots are lying straight up, and test the number of beads needed.

10. Pick up the number of beads determined in step 9. Sometimes, you may need to adjust this number by adding or leaving off one bead. Make these adjustments as needed so that the picots stand straight up and the row is lying properly on the cabochon. Stitch down through the top picot bead and up through the last added bead to create a loop (figure 9). Pull tightly to adjust the tension.

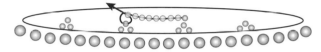

figure 9

11. Repeat step 10 around the cabochon.

12. When you reach the last section to close the loop, add only the number of beads between picots and not the one for the top of the picot, because that bead is already there.

13. Continue to stitch around and around the bezel row until the holes are filled with thread. This will strengthen the row and make the beads line up properly next to each other.

14. End near a picot. Stitch down through the picot beads and the under backing to the back side. Tie a knot, weave in the end, and cut the thread.

15. Thread a needle on the tail thread. Stitch down through the picot beads and the under backing to the back side. Tie a knot, weave in the end, and cut the thread.

Variation: You can produce a lovely variation of the picot bezel, called a diamond bezel, that provides a taller lift of the bezel row of beads and creates a beautiful geometric look. Use the instructions for the picot bezel, except when creating the picots, pick up four beads instead of three, and stitch back down through the first added bead (figure 10). Pull the thread to create the diamond shape. Add the top bezel row the same as you would for the picot bezel.

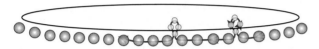

figure 10

Cabochon: **Fossil**
Bezel: **Diamond**
Edge: **Raw**
Attachment: **Top bail ladder**

the projects

You've learned how to make a basic beaded cabochon. You've read about (and perhaps even practiced) the various techniques for adding interesting edges, bezels, and other creative effects. Now it's time to apply what you've learned and start beading some beautiful cabochon jewelry.

All of the projects on the following pages are designed not only to create stunning pieces for you to wear or to give as gifts, but also to help you develop your skills. Choose a project, read the instructions, gather together the necessary materials, and jump right into the beading. Remember that patience and practice are always the keys to learning a new pursuit successfully.

By the time you've finished a few projects, you'll be well on your way to mastering the rewarding art and craft of beading with cabochons. And you'll be ready to explore the unlimited territory of designing your own jewelry; be sure to read chapter seven for advice on that subject.

fringed
dichroic glass
necklace

The metallic "fire" burning in this colorful cabochon is the hallmark of dichroic glass. By using large beads in the base row, you create a foundation for a raised bezel that emphasizes the cabochon's entrancing depth and sparkle.

What You Need
- Cabochon

 26 to 32 mm round dichroic glass cabochon, black background with turquoise blue and copper highlights

- Beads

 Seed Beads (approx. 10 grams of each color, or number of beads indicated)

 Size 5° or 6° round, turquoise AB finish (for base row)

 Size 15° round, copper-lined transparent (for bezel row, fringe, and points)

 Size 9° round, teal AB finish (for additional row and fringe)

 Size 11° round, opaque black (for edge row and fringe)

 Size 5° round, opaque black: 2

 Other Beads

 4 mm Capri blue faceted fire-polished round beads: 14

 4 mm teal round beads: 26

 5 mm Capri blue bicone beads: 30

 6 mm copper-lined transparent round beads: 30

 8 mm black faceted fire-polished round beads: 4

 3 x 6 mm black faceted wafer beads: 4

 2 x 4 mm black faceted bicone beads: 12

 6 mm black faceted fire-polished round beads: 36

- Beading thread, size A, black

- Beading needles, size 12 or 13
- Under backing material, $2\frac{1}{2}$ inches (6.4 cm) square
- Outer backing material, 2 inches (5.1 cm) square
- 4 gold jump rings, 5 mm
- Gold hook-and-eye clasp

Techniques Used
Bezel: **Bead-raised**
Edge: **Pointed with fringe**
Attachment: **Top loop**

Instructions
1. Using the dichroic glass cabochon, create a basic beaded cabochon by following the instructions in chapter two (page 15) through step 6, with the following variations:

- **Step 2 (page 16) variation:** Because dichroic glass cabochons have a fat edge, use size 5° or 6° beads instead of smaller beads for the base row. This will result in an elevation of the bezel row and compensate for the fat edge. See chapter five, page 61, for more about bead-raised bezels.
- **Step 3 (page 17) variation:** After you add the bezel row, add an additional row of beads outside the base row using size 9° seed beads. This will even out the slope of your finished cabochon and provide a trimmer appearance.

2. Using the top loop attachment instructions on page 57, create the top loops for attaching the necklace.

Fringe Chart

String the fringe strands as shown, following the bead key. (Note that the chart is designed to help you keep count of the beads in each strand and does not reflect the fringe's actual "V" shape outline)

Key

- Size 15° round seed bead, copper-lined transparent
- Size 9° round seed bead, teal AB finish
- Size 11° round seed bead, opaque black
- 4 mm Capri blue faceted fire-polished round bead
- 4 mm teal round bead
- 5 mm Capri blue bicone bead
- 6 mm copper-lined transparent round bead

Design Your Own Fringe

If you prefer to create your own fringe pattern rather than follow the chart, start by designing a central strand using 25 to 30 seed beads plus some larger décor beads at the bottom. Experiment with different combinations of bead colors and shapes. Try different lengths. Once you've settled on a length and a design, decide on the angle you want for the fringes. If you decrease the seed beads by two for every succeeding fringe from the center, the angle will be gentle. Decreasing by three, four, or five seed beads will create a sharper angle.

3. Now it's time to bead the fringe. Thread a needle with approximately 6 yards (5.46 m) of beading thread (this technique is worked single-thread). Starting at the bottom center from the back side, stitch up through the backings to the top side just above the center edge bead, between the edge row and the outer row. Pull the thread so that there are 3 yards (2.74 m) on the top side and 3 yards (2.74 m) on the back side. Stitch down through the center edge bead. You'll use the 3 yards (2.74 m) of thread on the needle to bead the center fringe strand and all the strands to the right. Later, you'll add a needle to the other 3 yards (2.74 m) of thread and use it to bead the fringe strands to the left of the center.

4. Using the fringe chart and the instructions in the fringes section of chapter three on page 44, add the fringes for the center strand and all the strands to the right. Then put a beading needle on the other 3 yards (2.74 m) of thread and add the fringe strands to the left of the center strand.

5. Using the pointed edge method instructions on page 29, stitch a pointed edge between the outermost fringe strand on each side and the top loops. As you complete the edge on each side, tie a knot in the thread strand, weave in the end, and cut.

STRINGING THE NECKLACE

6. Next, you'll string the necklace. Thread a needle with approximately 4 yards (3.66 m) of beading thread; this step is worked double-thread, so move the needle to the center of the thread to produce a double strand. Pick up 15 size 11° opaque black seed beads. Move the beads to the end of the thread, leaving a tail of approximately 9 inches (22.9 cm). Go through the beads again to create a loop. Then follow steps A through I below to create the necklace strand shown (or, of course, you can design your own).

    A. One size 5° round seed bead, opaque black

    B. One 6 mm black faceted fire-polished round bead and one size 11° round seed bead, opaque black

    C. Repeat step B 17 more times.

    D. One 2 x 4 mm black faceted bicone bead and one size 9° round seed bead, teal AB finish

    E. Repeat step D two more times.

    F. One 6 mm copper-lined transparent round bead, one 5 mm Capri blue bicone bead, one 3 x 6 mm black faceted wafer bead, and one 8 mm black faceted fire-polished round bead

    G. Repeat steps D through F.

    H. Pick up eight size 9° round seed beads, teal AB finish. Then put the necklace strand through the top loops of the beaded cabochon, and arrange the loops as needed to make them lie flat on the eight added beads.

    I. Repeat steps A through G, in reverse order and starting with the bead listed last in each step, to bead the other side of the strand.

7. Pick up 15 size 11° opaque black seed beads. Go through the beads again to create a loop. Pull the thread to adjust the tension of the strand.

8. Stitch back through all of the beads in the necklace strand. This will result in a total of four threads in the strand, giving it body and strength.

9. When you reach the end loop you created when you started stringing, tie the threads with a square knot, weave in the ends, and cut.

10. Use two jump rings though each end loop to attach the clasp findings to the necklace.

11. Congratulations. You've created a beautiful necklace!

Make Matching Earrings

You can easily make earrings to match your necklace. Just slip a few of the same beads you used in the fringe onto a pair of gold 2-inch (5.1 cm) headpins (straight wire findings with a flat knob at one end to hold the beads). After you've added the beads, use round-nose pliers to bend the "open" end of each headpin into a loop. Attach dangle wires or other earring findings to the loops.

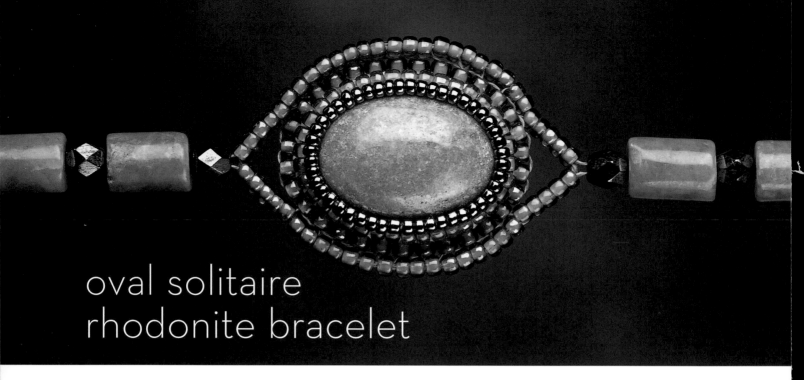

oval solitaire
rhodonite bracelet

This little bracelet is absolutely elegant in its simplicity and as feminine as the roses its color mimics. The turned bead edge serves two important functions: It provides a decorative frame for the cabochon, and it also makes the bracelet stronger.

What You Need
- Cabochon
  13 x 18 mm oval rhodonite cabochon
- Beads
  Seed Beads (approx. 10 grams of each color, or number of beads indicated)
    Size 11° round, rose pink (for base row, edge row, and bracelet)
    Size 15° round, dark metallic gray (for bezel row)
    Size 5° round, dark metallic gray (for end of bracelet): 2
  Other Beads
    4 mm dark metallic gray faceted fire-polished round beads: 10 to 12
    6 x 8 mm rhodonite tube beads: 8 to 10
- Beading thread, size A, pink
- Beading needles, size 12 or 13

- Under backing material, 1 x 1¼ inches (2.5 x 3.2 cm)
- Outer backing material, 1 x 1¼ inches (2.5 x 3.2 cm)
- 4 silver jump rings, 5 mm
- Silver toggle clasp, medium

Techniques Used
Bezel: **Standard**
Edge: **Turn bead**
Attachment: **Direct**

Instructions

1. Using the oval rhodonite cabochon, create a basic beaded cabochon by following the instructions in chapter two (page 15) through step 6, with the following variations:

• **Step 6 (page 22) variation:** For this project, the center beads are on the short sides of the oval. The actual center may be through a bead or it may be between two beads. Whichever is the case, make sure that each side is the same; in other words, if the center is between two beads on one side, use a between-beads center on the other side too. To accomplish this, you may need to have an uneven count, on the top versus the bottom, of edge beads between the centers. For this design, it's okay to make the top and bottom uneven, if necessary, to make sure the center beads are the same on each side (figure 1).

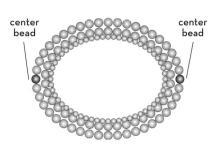

figure 1

2. Thread a needle with approximately 2 yards (1.83 m) of beading thread; this method is worked double-thread, so move the needle to the center to produce a double strand. Pick up nine size 11° rose pink round seed beads (figure 2). Go through the beads again and pull to create a loop, leaving a tail of approximately 9 inches (22.9 cm). See figure 3. Now pick up one size 5° dark metallic gray seed bead.

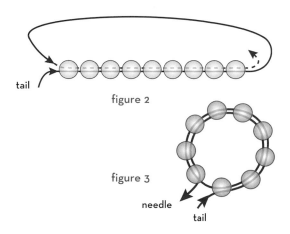

figure 2

figure 3

needle

tail

3. Pick up one 4 mm dark metallic gray faceted fire-polished bead and one 6 x 8 mm rhodonite tube bead. Move the beads toward the loop created in step 2.

4. Repeat step 3 until you have the bracelet length you want. Then add one final 4 mm dark metallic gray faceted fire-polished bead.

5. Pick up four size 11° rose pink seed beads. Stitch through the edge bead two beads up from the center beads, staying on the top side of the backings (figure 4).

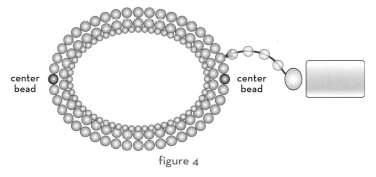

figure 4

6. Use a running stitch (page 37) to stitch over to the other side of the center beads, two beads over.

7. Stitch up through the edge bead and pick up four size 11° rose pink seed beads. Stitch though the 4 mm dark metallic gray faceted fire-polished bead and all the other beads on the bracelet strand (figure 5).

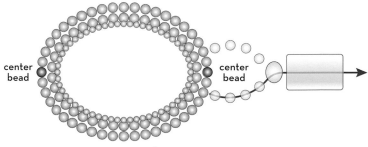

figure 5

8. After you stitch back through all the bracelet beads, you will return to the loop created in step 2. Tie the tail and needle-end threads with a square knot. Weave in the ends and cut.

9. Repeat steps 2 through 8 to create the other side of the bracelet.

10. Now it's time to add the turned bead edge. Thread a needle with approximately 1½ yards (1.37 m) of thread (this technique is worked single-thread). Stitch up from the back side to the top side between the edge row and the base row and through an edge bead that is near the bottom of the cabochon (figure 6). Follow the instructions for the turned bead edge stitch in chapter three, page 25.

figure 6

11. When you near the bracelet attachment, go through the seed beads used to attach the bracelet to the cabochon (figure 7).

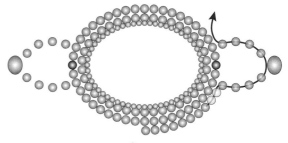

figure 7

12. Finish stitching the edge around the cabochon to the starting place. Then go back through the beads several times, filling the holes with thread to strengthen the edge and make the beads lie straighter by stitching again (and again) through the added turned bead edge beads and the seed beads where the bracelet is attached. Finally, stitch over to the back side near the original starting place. Tie the tail and needle-end threads with a square knot. Weave in the ends and cut.

13. Use two silver jump rings on each loop to attach the clasp.

noondrite jasper necklace

Shimmering gold-lined transparent seed beads circle the gemstone's center and crown the edge with tiny points of sparkle. Combining a variety of special techniques produces a spectacularly beaded cabochon; placing it on a simple strand of alternating beads emphasizes its regal appearance.

What You Need

- Cabochon
    - 38 mm round noondrite jasper cabochon
- Beads
    - Seed Beads (approx. 10 grams of each color, or number of beads indicated)
        - Size 11° round, matte opaque light brown (for bezel window, additional outer row and edge row)
        - Size 15° round, gold-lined transparent (for inside bezel row and points)
        - Size 5° round, bronze: 2
    - Other Beads
        - 7 x 15 mm noondrite twisted oval beads: 24
        - 4 mm green adventurine round beads: 54
- Beading thread, size A, light brown
- Beading needles, size 12 or 13
- Under backing material, 3 inches (7.6 cm) square
- Outer backing material, 2 ½ inches (6.4 cm) square
- 4 gold jump rings, 5 mm
- Gold hook-and-eye clasp

Techniques Used

Bezel: **Window**

Edge: **Pointed**

Attachment: **Turn bead**

Instructions

1. Using the noondrite jasper cabochon, create a basic beaded cabochon by following the instructions in chapter two (page 15) through step 6, with the following variations:

• Step 2 (page 16) variation: For the base row, use 32 of the 4 mm green adventurine round beads, and apply them with the couch stitch by following the instructions in the bead-raised bezel section of chapter five, beginning on page 000.

• Step 3 (page 16) first variation: When you add the bezel row, use the window bezel technique described in chapter five, page 64. This design uses two size 11° light brown seed beads for the height

of the window and one size 15° gold-lined transparent seed bead as the turn bead for the window. Space the windows along the base row every two beads. Use size 15° gold-lined transparent seed beads for the top of the window bezel row. See illustrations 4 and 5 in chapter five, page 65.

• Step 3 (page 17) second variation: After you've added the bezel, stitch an additional outer row around the base row using size 11° light brown seed beads. See the instructions for optional step H in chapter two, page 19.

2. After you've finished the variations and then completed the cabochon by following the directions for steps 4 through 6 of the basic beaded cabochon (pages 19 through 22), you'll be ready to stitch on the turn beads. Thread a needle with 2 ½ yards (2.29 m) of beading thread (this step and the next are worked single-thread). Following the instructions for the turn bead attachment method in chapter four, beginning on page 50, apply the turn beads. Use either three or four size 11° light brown seed beads, whichever will leave an even number of empty edge beads. Once you've sewn on the beads, tie the threads with a square knot but do not cut them.

3. Using the same thread and the instructions for the pointed edge method in chapter two, beginning on page 29, apply the points for the edge. When you've completed all the points, stitch over to the tail thread using a running stitch, as illustrated on page 37. Tie the threads with a square knot, weave in the ends, and cut.

STRINGING THE NECKLACE

4. You've finished beading the cabochon, so now it's time to string the necklace. Thread a needle with approximately 4 yards (3.66 m) of beading thread; this step is worked double-thread, so move the needle to the center of the thread to produce a double strand. Pick up one size 5° bronze seed bead. Move the bead to the end of the thread and loop the thread around it to create a stop bead, leaving a tail of approximately 9 inches (22.9 cm). Then follow steps A through E below, picking up beads as indicated, to string the necklace strand shown (or, of course, you can design your own).

- **A.** One 7 x 15 mm noondrite twisted oval bead and one 4 mm green adventurine bead
- **B.** Repeat step A 10 more times so that you've strung a total of 11 pairs of beads.
- **C.** One 7 x 15 mm noondrite twisted oval bead and one size 11° light brown seed bead
- **D.** Stitch through the turn beads on the beaded cabochon.
- **E.** Repeat steps A through C, in reverse order and starting with the bead listed last in each step, to bead the other side of the strand.

5. Pick up one size 5° bronze seed bead and 13 size 11° light brown seed beads. Go back through the 13 size 11° seed beads to create a loop.

6. Stitch back through all the beads in the necklace strand to the starting point.

7. Remove the loop thread from the stop bead and stitch through that bead.

8. Pick up 13 size 11° light brown seed beads. Stitch back through the same size 11° seed beads to create a loop. Pull the thread to adjust the tension of the strand.

9. Tie the threads with a square knot, weave in the ends, and cut.

10. Use two jump rings through each end loop to attach the hook clasp at one end and the eye portion of the clasp at the other end. You're done!

sea moss
ladder
bracelet

The connected double strands of this dainty bracelet's "ladder" add interest without stealing the show from the true focal point, a lovely rhyolite gemstone flanked by unakite beads. Combining cabochons and the ladder stitch gives you almost unlimited versatility for bracelet designs.

What You Need

- Cabochon
    15 mm round rhyolite cabochon
- Beads
    Seed Beads (approx. 10 grams of each color, or number of beads indicated)
        Size 11° round, light green (for base row, edge row, points, and bracelet)
        Size 15° round, metallic bronze (for bezel row)
        Size 9° round, metallic bronze (for bracelet)
        Size 5° round, metallic bronze (for end of bracelet): 2
    Other Beads
        6 mm unakite round beads: 3
        3 x 5 mm unakite tube beads: 10 to 12
- Beading thread, size A, olive green
- Beading needles, size 12 or 13
- Under backing material, 1¼ inches (3.2 cm) square
- Outer backing material, 1 inch (2.5 cm) square
- 3 gold jump rings, 5 mm
- Gold lobster-claw clasp
- Gold chain, 2 inches (5.1 cm) long
- Gold headpin, 1 inch (2.5 cm) long
- Wire cutters
- Round-nose pliers

Techniques Used

Bezel: **Standard**
Edge: **Pointed**
Attachment: **Direct**

Instructions

1. Using the rhyolite cabochon, create a basic beaded cabochon by following the instructions in chapter two (page 15) through step 5, "Bead the Basic Edge." For this project, use 32 size 11° light green seed beads for the basic edge.

2. Next, you'll locate and mark the center beads on the sides of the cabochon where the bracelet beads will be attached. For this design, each center needs to be between two beads, not through a bead. Tie a thread through two adjacent beads on one side— where you want that center to be—to serve as a temporary marking. Now, starting with the first edge bead after a marked bead, count around the edge 14 beads. The next two edge beads should be the center beads on the other side. Put a needle in each of these two beads to mark them temporarily. Now count the edge beads between the marked beads on both sides to make sure the counts are the same. In this project, the total on each side between the pairs of center beads should be 14. Once you've verified that the counts are the same, remove the needles from the two beads on the other side and tie a thread through them as a temporary marker.

3. The stitch used to create the bracelet is a two-needle ladder stitch. Thread a needle with approximately 2 yards (1.83 m) of beading thread; this method is worked double-thread, so move the needle to the center to produce a double strand. Stitch up through the backings from the back side to the beaded cabochon top. Enter two beads over from the center beads, between the base row and the edge bead row. Stitch up through that edge bead. Leave a tail on the back side of approximately 9 inches (22.9 cm).

4. Now cut another 2 yards (1.83 m) of thread, moving the needle to the center to produce a double strand. Repeat the stitching in step 3, except enter two beads over from the other side of the center beads. You will now have two needles and thread on the same side of the bracelet coming out of edge beads that have four beads between them.

5. On one needle, pick up three size 11° light green seed beads, one size 9° metallic bronze seed bead, one 6 mm unakite round bead, and one more size 9° metallic bronze seed bead.

6. With the other needle, pick up three size 11° light-green seed beads, and stitch through the size 9° metallic bronze seed beads and 6 mm unakite round bead from step 5. Pull both needles to center the size 9° seeds and 6 mm round (figure 1).

7. Now, on one needle pick up three size 11° light green seed beads, one size 9° metallic bronze seed bead, one 3 x 5 mm unakite tube bead, and one more size 9° metallic bronze seed bead.

8. With the other needle, pick up three size 11° light-green seed beads and stitch through the size 9° metallic bronze seed beads and 3 x 5 mm unakite tube from step 7. Pull both needles to center the size 9° metallic bronze seed bead and 3 x 5 mm unakite tube beads (figure 2).

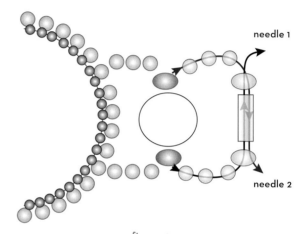

figure 2

9. Repeat steps 7 and 8 until you have the desired length for this half of the bracelet.

10. On one needle, pick up four size 11° light green seed beads and one size 5° metallic bronze seed bead. With the other needle, pick up four size 11° light green seed beads and stitch through the size 5° seed bead on the other thread.

11. Select one needle, and pick up nine size 11° light green seed beads. Move the seeds all the way down to the size 5° metallic bronze bead. Go through the same beads again to create a loop. Pull the thread and position the beads so that the loop is next to the size 5° metallic bronze seed bead (figure 3).

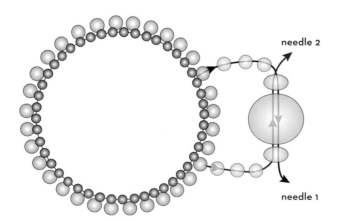

figure 1

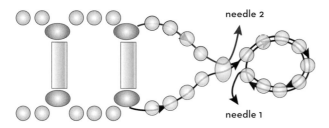

figure 3

12. With the other needle, go through the loop again, but enter from the side opposite that used by the other thread. Pull and adjust the thread to the proper tension. Tie the two threads together with a square knot.

13. With one thread, go back through the four size 11° light green seed beads next to the size 5° metallic bronze seed bead. With the other needle, go through the other four size 11° light green seed beads.

14. Stitch back through the sides of the ladder, one needle on each side. Add one size 11° light green seed bead at each intersection of a ladder rung (figure 4). Stitch all the way back to the cabochon.

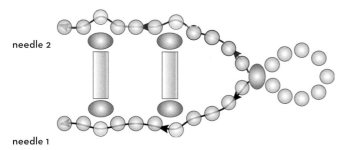

figure 4

15. Stitch through the edge bead on the cabochon, staying on the top side of the backings. Then stitch down to the back side.

16. Tie a square knot on each side using the needle-end threads and tail threads on each side. Weave in the ends and cut.

17. Repeat steps 3 through 16 to create the other side of the bracelet.

18. Thread a needle with approximately 1 yard (.91 m) of beading thread (this technique is worked single-thread).

19. From the back side, stitch up to the top side next to an edge bead near the bracelet ladder.

20. Stitch up through the edge bead.

21. Using the pointed edge method instructions on page 29, add points to the edge until you reach the bracelet ladder on the opposite side. Then use small up-and-down stitches through the backing, stitching between the edge row and the base row, until you get past the bracelet ladder. Now add the points on the other side.

22. Stitch over to the tail thread and tie a square knot. Weave in the ends and cut.

23. Use one jump ring to attach the clasp to one end and two jump rings side by side to attach the chain to the other end.

24. Put one 6 mm round unakite bead on the headpin. With the wire cutters, trim the headpin to ¼ inch (6 mm) above the bead. Using the pliers, bend that portion into a loop over the chain end.

double
cabochon
dangle
earrings

Subtly linked cabochons, each surrounded by a starburst of tiny foil-lined seed beads, are punctuated by a single dangling drop bead. Because the round cabochons are so small, the base row also serves as a bezel row to hold the stones in place.

What You Need
• Cabochons
  - 13 x 18 mm oval unakite cabochons: 2
  - 8 mm round Malaysian jade cabochons, dyed dark peach: 2
• Beads
  - Seed Beads (approx. 10 grams of each color, or number of beads indicated)
    - Size 11° round, matte transparent olive green (for base row on oval cabochons and for all edge rows)
    - Size 15° round, metallic olive green (for bezel row and drop fringe on oval cabochons)
    - Size 11° round, metallic olive green (for base row on round cabochons and drop fringe on oval cabochons)
    - Size 15° round, foil-lined dark peach (for points on edge)
  - Other Beads
    - 6 mm round unakite beads: 2
• Beading thread, size A, olive green
• Beading needles, size 12 or 13
• 4 pieces of under backing material, each 1 inch (2.5 cm) square
• 4 pieces of outer backing material, each 1 inch (2.5 cm) square
• 2 gold ear wires

Techniques Used
Bezel: **Standard**
Edge: **Pointed with fringe drops**
Attachment: **Direct**

Instructions
1. Using the oval unakite cabochons, create basic beaded cabochons by following the instructions in chapter two (page 15) through step 6. Remember to keep track of the number of beads used in each row on the cabochon so that you can duplicate it on the second cabochon (see the sidebar on page 86).

2. Using the round cabochons, create basic beaded cabochons by following the instructions in chapter two (page 15) through step 6, with the following variations:

• **Step 3 (page 17) variation:** Skip this step; in other words, don't apply a bezel row. Because the 8 mm round cabochons are so small, the base row will do double duty and also act as the bezel row. See the section "Working with Small Cabochons" on page 106 of chapter seven.

3. You should now have four beaded cabochons with the center beads marked. Match up one round cabochon with an oval cabochon for one of the earrings. Match up the other round with the other oval for the second earring.

4. To attach the oval cabochon to the round cabochon, read the instructions for the direct attachment method on page 47. Although the instructions relate to attaching a necklace to a beaded cabochon, the same process can be used to attach one beaded cabochon to another. To start, thread a needle with approximately 1 yard (.91 m) of beading thread (this technique is worked single-thread). Then align the center beads on the bottom of the round cabochon with the center beads on the top of the oval cabochon.

5. On the oval cabochon, stitch up through the backings from the back side between the base row and the edge row, just under one of the center beads.

6. Stitch through the center edge bead on the oval cabochon.

7. Stitch through the center edge bead on the round cabochon, staying on the back side of the backings. Pull the thread until the edge beads on both cabochons meet; leave a tail on the oval cabochon of approximately 9 inches (22.9 cm).

8. Stitch up through the backings to the top side of the round cabochon, just above the center edge bead, between the base row and the edge row.

9. Stitch over to the next center bead by stitching down to the back side between the base row and the edge row.

10. Stitch to the oval cabochon through the center edge beads on both the round and the oval cabochons. Stay on the back side of the backings.

11. Stitch up to the top side of the oval cabochon above the center bead between the base row and the edge row.

12. Stitch over to the first center bead by stitching down to the back side between the base row and the edge row.

13. Repeat steps 6 through 12 to strengthen and reinforce the attachment.

14. Tie the tail and needle-end threads with a square knot, weave in the ends, and cut.

15. Repeat steps 4 through 14 for the second earring.

16. Now it's time to create a loop for attaching one earring's gold ear wire finding. Thread a needle with approximately 2 yards (1.83 m) of beading thread (this technique is worked single-thread). Then follow the instructions for attaching dangle earring findings on page 119, starting with step 2 and ending with step 11. Space each loop one or two beads apart as needed to center the earring's round cabochon. *Do not tie off the thread once the loops are done.*

17. Using the same thread that you used in step 16, start the edge stitching next to the loop you just made, following the instructions for the pointed

18. Continue adding beads down the oval cabochon using the pointed edge stitch. When you near the bottom center, create the drop-bead fringe. Depending on your edge bead count, there will be one or two edge beads between the two connecting points for the fringe loop and the bottom center edge bead (refer to the project photo). Pick up three size 15° metallic olive green seed beads, one size 11° metallic olive green seed bead, one 6 mm unakite round bead, and one size 15° metallic olive green seed bead. Now you'll go back through some, but not all, of the same beads. Skip the last size 15° metallic olive green seed bead you added and stitch back up through the 6 mm unakite round bead and the size 11° metallic olive green seed bead. Pull the thread to adjust the tension. Then pick up three size 15° metallic olive green seed beads, and stitch up through the edge bead to connect the fringe on the opposite side, staying on the back side. Stitch up to the top side between the base row and the edge row, just above the edge bead.

19. Continue stitching on the pointed edge, back to the top, duplicating on this side the same pattern created on the first side.

20. Use a running stitch to stitch over to the tail thread. Tie the threads with a square knot, weave in the ends, and cut.

21. Repeat steps 16 through 20 for the other earring.

edge method in chapter three, page 29. Continue down the round cabochon. When you reach the point where the two cabochons meet, stitch over to the oval cabochon through the center beads where the two cabochons are attached.

leopardskin
jasper
necklace

Entwined strands of black and gold edge beads spiral around this earth-toned necklace's spotted gemstone. The simple but elegant picot bezel creates lacy windows that embellish the cabochon without covering it.

What You Need
- Cabochon
    30 to 35 mm round leopardskin jasper cabochon
- Beads
    Seed Beads (approx. 10 grams of each color, or number of beads indicated)
        Size 11° round, white-lined brown transparent (for base row and two-bead edge)
        Size 15° round, black (for bezel picots and twisted edge)
        Size 15° round, bronze (for bezel row and twisted edge)
        Size 5° round, opaque black: 2
        Size 11° round, opaque black: 2
    Other Beads
        4 mm opaque black round beads: 38
        8 mm leopardskin jasper round beads: 16
        6 mm tiger jasper round beads: 6
        8 mm tiger jasper round beads: 16
- Beading thread, size A, brown
- Beading needles, size 12 or 13
- Under backing material, 2 inches (5.1 cm) square
- Outer backing material, 2 inches (5.1 cm) square
- 4 gold jump rings, 5 mm
- Gold chain, 4 inches (10.2 cm) long
- Gold hook clasp
- Gold headpin, 1 ½ inches (3.8 cm) long
- Wire cutters
- Round-nose pliers

Techniques Used
Bezel: **Picot**
Edge: **Twisted**
Attachment: **Turn bead**

Instructions
1. Using the leopardskin jasper cabochon, create a basic beaded cabochon by following the instructions in chapter two (page 15) through step 6, with the following variations:

- **Step 3 (page 17) variation:** When you add the bezel row, use the picot bezel technique described in chapter five, beginning on page 66.
- **Step 5 (page 20) variation:** Instead of the basic edge, use the two-bead edge variation described in chapter two, beginning on page 21.

2. Next, create the twisted edge, following the instructions in chapter three, beginning on page 32. Each of the two strands in the twisted edge is a different color, so when you add the picot beads around the cabochon, alternate the bead colors, first using a black size 15° seed bead, then a bronze (or vice versa, as you prefer), and so forth. Likewise, when you add beads of one color for the first twisted strand, make sure the color matches that of the first picot bead you'll stitch through.

Remember that this type of edge technique calls for a repeating pattern. If your cabochon's edge count isn't evenly divisible by the pattern count, you can solve the problem by starting the edge stitch at the spot where you want the top of the cabochon to be. You can then make the twists longer or shorter in that area to compensate without compromising your design. When you complete the twisted strands, tie the ends with a square not but do not weave in and cut the thread.

3. Using size 11° white-lined brown transparent seed beads and the thread ends from the previous step, follow the instructions for the turn bead attachment method in chapter four, on page 50, to apply the beads used to attach the necklace. The attachment for this design requires only two turn beads. Once you've sewn on the beads, tie the threads with a square knot, weave in the ends, and cut.

STRINGING THE NECKLACE

4. Now you're ready to string the necklace. Thread a needle with approximately 4 yards (3.66 m) of beading thread; this step is worked double-thread, so move the needle to the center of the thread to produce a double strand. Pick up 15 size 11° white-lined brown transparent seed beads. Move the beads to the end of the thread, leaving a tail of approximately 9 inches (22.9 cm). Go through the beads again to create a loop. Then follow steps A through J below, picking up beads as indicated, to string the necklace strand shown (or, of course, you can design your own).

A. One size 5° round seed bead, opaque black

B. One 4 mm opaque black round bead and one 6 mm tiger jasper round bead

C. Repeat step B.

D. One 4 mm opaque black round bead, one 8 mm leopardskin jasper round bead, and one 4 mm opaque black round bead

E. One 8 mm tiger jasper round bead

F. Repeat steps D and E six more times.

G. Repeat step D.

H. One 6 mm tiger jasper round bead, one 4 mm opaque black round bead, and one size 11° round seed bead, opaque black

I. Stitch through the turn beads on the beaded cabochon.

J. Repeat steps A through H, in reverse order and starting with the bead listed last in each step, to bead the other side of the strand.

5. Pick up 15 size 11° white-lined brown transparent seed beads. Stitch through the beads again to create a loop. Pull the thread to adjust the tension of the strand.

6. Stitch back through all the beads in the necklace strand. This will result in a total of four threads in the strand, giving it body and strength.

7. When you reach the end loop you created when you started stringing, tie the threads with a square knot, weave in the ends, and cut.

8. Use two jump rings through each end loop to attach the hook clasp at one end and the chain at the other end.

9. Place one 8 mm tiger jasper round bead, and then one 4 mm opaque black round bead, onto the headpin.

10. If necessary, trim the end of the headpin using the wire cutters. Then, with the pliers, bend the "open" end of the headpin into a loop through the last link in the chain. You're done!

black
onyx
pin

This piece combines classic black-and-gold evening chic with a whimsical flowerlike scalloped edge and leafy fringe. The number of fringe strands depends on the number of beads left empty after you've added the scallops.

What You Need

- Cabochon
  - 20 to 25 mm round black onyx cabochon
- Beads
  - Seed Beads (approx. 10 grams of each color, or the number of beads indicated)
    - Size 11° round, black-lined gold (for base and edge rows)
    - Size 15° round, metallic gold (for bezel row)
    - Size 5° round, metallic gold: 1 to 3
    - Size 15° round, black: 1 to 3
  - Other Beads
    - 4 mm black round beads: 12 to 16
    - 4 x 6 mm black faceted wafer beads: 1 to 3
    - Black leaf beads: 1 to 3
- Permanent marker, black
- Beading thread, size A, black
- Beading needles, size 12 or 13
- Under backing material, 2 inches (5.1 cm) square
- Tie-tack-style pin finding, with pad at least 10 mm wide
- Piece of plastic cut from an empty plastic milk jug
- Scissors
- Flexible glue
- Heavy-duty glue
- Outer backing material, 2 inches (5.1 cm) square

Techniques Used

Bezel: **Standard**

Edge: **Scalloped**

Attachment: **Fringe**

Instructions

1. Using the permanent marker, color the under backing black so that it will not contrast with the cabochon and beads.

2. Using the black onyx cabochon, create a basic beaded cabochon by following the instructions in chapter two (page 15) through step 3. Then trim the under backing as described in part A of chapter two's step 4 (page 19). *Do not go on to attach the outer backing yet.*

3. Now attach the pin finding as described in the "Attaching Tie-Tack-Style and Stickpin Findings" section of the Appendix, on page 122. Be sure to apply the piece of plastic, as directed, over the finding pad to reinforce the attachment.

4. After you've attached the finding and the outer backing, follow the instructions for beading a basic edge in chapter two's step 5 (page 20).

5. Now, by following the instructions starting on page 41, create the pin's scalloped edge. Using the 4 mm black round beads for the center beads, and the size 11° black-lined gold seed beads for the scallops, should result in one full scallop for every three edge beads. Start the process near the bottom of the pin.

6. Continue stitching scallops around the edge. As you near the starting point at the bottom, determine how many edge beads will be left after the last scallop. There are three possibilities. The number of edge beads left can be one, two, or three. Add a fringe strand to each of the empty edge beads. If there is only one edge bead left and you want a fuller fringe, use a branch fringe technique as shown in the photo. See chapter three, page 44, for instructions on how to attach fringe. Start each strand with several size 11° black-lined gold seed beads, depending on your design, and end each strand with the following sequence: one size 5° gold seed bead, one 4 x 6 mm black faceted wafer bead, one black leaf bead, and one size 15° black seed bead.

victorian triple
cabochon bracelet

Engraved Bali silver accent beads and a trio of sparkling amethyst cabochons recall
an era of epic romances and jewelry to match. This bracelet only looks complicated;
connecting the cabochons to one another and to the bracelet strands couldn't be simpler.

What You Need

- Cabochon
    15 mm round amethyst cabochons: 3
- Beads
    Seed Beads (approx. 10 grams of each color,
    or number of beads indicated)
        Size 11° round, purple transparent
        (for base row, edge row, and bracelet)
        Size 15° round, metallic silver
        (for bezel row and points)
        Size 5° round, metallic silver
        (for end of bracelet): 2
    Other Beads
        5 mm amethyst round beads: 32
        4 mm Bali silver round beads: 2
        2 mm Bali silver spacer beads: 4

- Beading thread, size A, purple
- Beading needles, size 12 or 13
- 3 pieces of under backing material, each 1 1/4 inches
    (3.2 cm) square
- 3 pieces of outer backing material, each 1 1/4 inches
    (3.2 cm) square
- 4 silver jump rings, 5 mm
- Silver toggle clasp, medium

Techniques Used
Bezel: **Standard**
Edge: **Pointed**
Attachments: **Direct and turn bead**

Instructions

1. Using the round amethyst cabochons, create three basic beaded cabochons by following the instructions in chapter two (page 15), through step 5, "Bead the Basic Edge." For this project, use 30 size 11° purple transparent seed beads for the basic edge on each cabochon.

2. Thread a needle with approximately 2 yards (1.83 m) of thread (this technique is worked single-thread). Take one of the cabochons and stitch up through the backings from the back side to the top side, stitching between the base row and the edge row; leave a tail of approximately 9 inches (22.9 cm). Stitch out through the edge bead.

3. Pick up one 5 mm amethyst round bead, one 4 mm Bali silver round bead, and another 5 mm amethyst round bead. Stitch through the edge bead of a second cabochon, staying on the top side. Stitch down through the backings to the back side. Stitch back out through the edge bead and the added amethyst round and Bali silver beads, then back through the edge bead on the original cabochon. Stay on the top side when stitching through the edge bead. Now stitch down through the backings to the back side (figure 1).

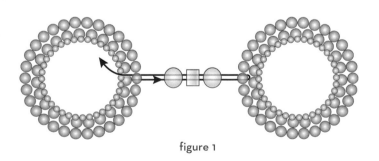

figure 1

4. Stitch over to the next edge bead. Following the instructions for the pointed edge method in chapter three, page 29, stitch on two edge points. Skip the next edge bead by sewing past it, using a running stitch (illustrated on page 37). Then, following the instructions for the turn bead attachment method in

chapter four, page 50, apply three added beads over the next four edge beads to create a turn bead attachment. Skip the next edge bead (again, sew past it, using a running stitch). Stitch on two edge points. Skip the next edge bead and stitch on two more edge points. Skip the next edge bead. Use three added beads over the next four beads to create a turn bead attachment. Skip the next edge bead and finish the circle with two more edge points (figure 2).

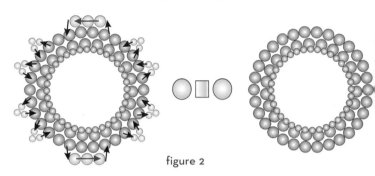

figure 2

5. Stitch over to the next edge bead. This is the bead you used to attach the 5 mm amethyst and 4 mm Bali silver beads to the second cabochon. The tail thread is here. Tie the thread ends with a square knot. Using a needle on the tail thread, weave in the end and cut.

6. Stitch back through the 5 mm amethyst round bead and 4 mm Bali silver round bead to the other cabochon. Repeat step 4 to create the edge on this second cabochon.

7. When you complete the edge on the second cabochon, your needle and thread will be close to the edge bead where the 5 mm amethyst and 4 mm Bali silver beads are attached. Again using a running stitch, stitch over to the bead directly opposite (15 edge beads over).

8. Stitch through the edge bead. Pick up one 5 mm amethyst round bead, one 4 mm Bali silver round bead, and one more 5 mm amethyst round bead. Stitch through an edge bead on the third cabochon, staying on the top side. Stitch through the backings to the back side.

9. Now stitch back up through the edge bead, and back through the amethyst and Bali silver beads you just added, to the second cabochon, staying on the top side. Stitch through the backings to the back side.

10. Stitch back up through that edge bead, and back through the amethyst and Bali silver beads, to the third cabochon. This will make a total of three threads through the amethyst and Bali silver beads. Now stitch from the top side down through the backings to the back side.

11. Repeat step 4 on the third cabochon. Stitch to the back side. Tie the thread, weave in the end, and cut.

12. Thread a needle with approximately 2 yards (1.83 m) of beading thread; this portion of the project is worked double-thread, so move the needle to the center to produce a double strand. Pick up nine size 11° purple transparent seed beads. Go through the beads again (figure 3) and pull the thread to create a loop (figure 4), leaving a tail of approximately 9 inches (22.9 cm). Pick up one size 5° metallic silver seed bead.

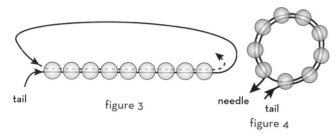

tail

figure 3

needle

tail

figure 4

13. Pick up four size 11° purple transparent seed beads, three 5 mm amethyst round beads, one Bali silver spacer bead, one 5 mm amethyst round bead, and five size 11° purple transparent seed beads. Move the beads toward the loop created in the previous step.

14. Stitch through the turn beads on the first cabochon.

15. Pick up five size 11° purple transparent seed beads, three 5 mm amethyst round beads, and five more size 11° purple transparent seed beads. Stitch through the turn beads on the middle cabochon.

The cabochons should lie even and straight. If they don't, remove one of the size 11° purple transparent seed beads, or add another, as needed (figure 5).

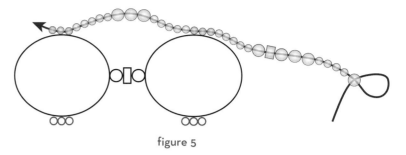

figure 5

16. Repeat step 15 from the middle cabochon to the last cabochon.

17. Pick up five size 11° purple transparent seed beads, one 5 mm amethyst round bead, one 2 mm Bali silver spacer bead, three 5 mm amethyst round beads, and four size 11° purple transparent beads.

18. To create the loop on this end, pick up one size 5° metallic silver seed bead and nine size 11° purple transparent seed beads. Stitch back through the nine seed beads and pull the thread to adjust the tension as needed.

19. Repeat steps 13 through 17 for the other side, and return to the first created loop.

20. Tie the tail threads and needle threads with a square knot. Weave in the ends and cut.

21. Use two silver jump rings on each loop to attach the clasp.

southwest
spirit
necklace

Bold coral sticks and turquoise Heishe beads evoke the spirit and beauty of the American Southwest's red-rock canyon country. Using turquoise for every fourth seed bead in the base row creates colorful accents for the malachite cabochon.

What You Need
- Cabochon
    - 30 x 40 mm oval red malachite cabochon
- Beads
    - Seed Beads (approx. 10 grams of each color, or number of beads indicated)
        - Size 11° round, matte opaque dark brownish-red (for base row and edge row)
        - Size 11° round, opaque turquoise (for base row accents)
        - Size 15° round, bronze (for bezel row)
        - Size 5° round, bronze: 3
        - Size 9° round, bronze: 2
    - Other Beads
        - 6 mm bronze round beads: 25
        - 4 x 9 mm turquoise Heishe beads: 53
        - 1¼-inch-long (3.2 cm) coral sticks, center-drilled: 14
- Beading thread, size A, brown
- Beading needles, size 12 or 13
- Under backing material, 2 x 2½ inches (6.4 cm)
- Outer backing material, 2 x 2½ inches (6.4 cm)
- 4 gold jump rings, 5 mm
- Gold chain, 4 inches (10.2 cm) long
- Gold hook clasp
- Gold headpin, 1½ inches (3.8 cm) long
- Wire cutters
- Round-nose pliers

Techniques Used
Bezel: **Standard**
Edge: **Raw**
Attachment: **Turn bead**

Instructions

1. Using the red malachite cabochon, create a basic beaded cabochon by following the instructions in chapter two (page 15) through step 6, with the following variation:

   • **Step 3 (page 17) variation:** For each sequence of four beads, use three size 11° brownish-red seed beads followed by one size 11° turquoise seed bead.

2. Using the two size 9° bronze seed beads and the instructions for the turn bead attachment method in chapter four, beginning on page 50, stitch the turn beads into place on the cabochon.

STRINGING THE NECKLACE

3. Now you can string the necklace. Thread a needle with approximately 4½ yards (4.11 m) of beading thread; this step is worked double-thread, so move the needle to the center of the thread to produce a double strand. Pick up one size 5° bronze seed bead. Move the bead to the end of the thread and loop the thread around it to create a stop bead, leaving a tail of approximately 9 inches (22.9 cm). Then follow steps A through G below, picking up beads as indicated, to string the necklace strand shown (or, of course, you can design your own).

   A. One 6 mm bronze round bead and three 4 x 9 mm turquoise Heishe beads

   B. Repeat step A two more times.

   C. One 6 mm bronze round bead, one 4 x 9 mm turquoise Heishe bead, one 1¼-inch-long coral stick, and one 4 x 9 mm turquoise Heishe bead

   D. Repeat step C six more times.

   E. One 6 mm bronze round bead, three 4 x 9 mm turquoise Heishe beads, and one 6 mm bronze round bead

   F. Stitch through the turn beads on the beaded cabochon.

   G. Repeat steps A through E, in reverse order and starting with the bead listed last in each step, to bead the other side of the strand.

4. Pick up one size 5° bronze seed bead and 13 size 11° brownish-red seed beads. Go back through the 13 size 11° seed beads to create a loop.

5. Stitch back through all the beads in the necklace strand to the starting point.

6. Remove the loop thread from the stop bead and stitch through that bead.

7. Pick up 13 size 11° brownish-red seed beads. Stitch back through the same size 11° seed beads to create a loop. Pull the thread to adjust the tension of the strand.

8. Tie the threads with a square knot, weave in the ends, and cut.

9. Attach two jump rings to each end loop; then attach the hook clasp to the rings at one end and the chain to the rings at the other end.

10. Place one 6 mm bronze round bead, one 4 x 9 mm turquoise Heishe bead, and one size 5° bronze seed bead onto the headpin.

11. If necessary, trim the end of the headpin using the wire cutters. Then, with the pliers, bend the "open" end of the headpin into a loop through the last link in the chain.

fringed tiger-eye cabochon earrings

Lavishly fringed tiger-eye cabochons gaze beneath arched golden "brows," echoing the imperial designs of Cleopatra's day. Each fringe strand is identical except for the number of initial seed beads.

What You Need

- Cabochons
    - 13 x 18 mm oval tiger-eye cabochons: 2
- Beads
    - Seed Beads (approx. 10 grams of each color, or number of beads indicated)
        - Size 11° round, brown-lined transparent green (for base row, edge row, and fringe)
        - Size 15° round, metallic gold (for bezel row and points)
    - Other Beads
        - Size 3° bronze bugle beads: 26
        - 4 mm olive green fire-polished round beads: 26
        - 5 mm tiger-eye round beads: 26
- Beading thread, size A, light brown
- Beading needles, size 12 or 13
- 2 pieces of under backing material, each 1 x 1½ inches (2.5 x 3.8 cm)
- 2 pieces of plastic cut from an empty milk carton
- 2 post backings, with 10 mm pads
- 2 pieces of outer backing material, each 1 inch (2.5 cm) square

Techniques Used

Bezel: **Standard**
Edge: **Points, fringe**

Instructions

1. Using the oval tiger-eye cabochons, create two basic beaded cabochons by following the instructions in chapter two (page 15) through step 3. Then trim the under backings as described in part A of chapter two's step 4 (page 19). *Do not go on to attach the outer backings yet.*

2. Because this design calls for a detailed edge and fringe, it's best to add the edging after you've attached the post findings and outer backings. Follow the instructions in "Attaching Post Findings for Button Earrings" in the Appendix, on page 120. Glue each ear post to its cabochon and then apply the outer backings, as detailed in steps 3 through 6 of that section, on page 121. (Because the cabochons are relatively large, be sure to add a plastic backing, using the pieces of plastic cut from a milk carton).

3. Once the glue is dry, finish making the two basic beaded cabochons by completing step 5 ("Bead the Basic Edge") and step 6 ("Mark the Center Beads") in chapter two (pages 20 through 22).

4. Now you'll add the fringe. Thread a needle with approximately 3 yards (2.74 m) of beading thread (this step is worked single-thread). From the back side, stitch up through the backings above the cabochon's bottom center bead. Stitch through the center edge bead. Pull the thread so that the tail is approximately 1½ yards (1.37 m) long.

5. Stitch on the fringe, starting in the center and working the fringe to the right, based on the chart on page 101. Refer to chapter four (page 44) for more on fringe attachments. After all fringes to the right are done, put a needle on the tail thread and use that thread to stitch on the fringes to the left.

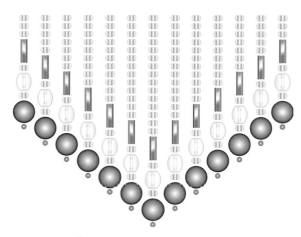

Fringe Chart

String the fringe strands as shown, following the bead key.

Key

 Size 11° round seed bead, brown-lined transparent green

Size 3° bronze bugle bead

4 mm olive green fire-polished round bead

5 mm tiger-eye round bead

 Size 15° round seed bead, metallic gold

6. Now, using the needle and thread on the right and the instructions for the pointed edge method on page 29 of chapter three, apply a pointed edge to the right half of the cabochon, all the way around to the top center bead.

7. Next, use the needle and thread on the left to apply a pointed edge around the left side of the cabochon to the top center bead.

8. Tie the threads with a square knot, weave in the ends, and cut.

9. Repeat steps 4 through 8 with the other cabochon.

crazy lace
agate pin

This subtly designed contemporary pin features a spectacular rippled cabochon showcased in a framework of simple rows that match the stone's colors. You could make this pin dozens of times and each would be unique, because every cabochon is different.

What You Need

- Cabochon
    - 40 x 30 mm oval crazy lace agate cabochon
- Seed Beads (approx. 10 grams of each color)
    - Size 11° round, red (for base row)
    - Size 15° round, dark gray (for bezel row)
    - Size 11° round, gray (for edge row)
    - Size 11° round, dark gray (for picots on edge row)
- Beading thread, size A, beige
- Beading needle, size 12 or 13
- Under backing material, 2 x 2½ inches (5.1 x 6.4 cm)
- Heavy-duty adhesive
- Piece of sheet metal flashing, 2 x 2½ inches (5.1 x 6.4 cm)
- Tin snips or heavy-duty scissors
- Bar pin finding, 1 inch (2.5 cm) long
- Outer backing material, 2 x 2½ inches (5.1 x 6.4 cm)

Techniques Used

Bezel: **Standard**

Edge: **Standard with picot variation**

Instructions

1. Using the crazy lace agate cabochon, create a basic beaded cabochon as detailed in chapter two (page 15) through step 3. Then trim the under backing as described in part A of chapter two's step 4 (page 19). *Do not go on to attach the outer backing yet.*

2. Because this design calls for only a simple picot edge, you can do the edge beading on the under backing before attaching the finding and outer backing. Stitch the edge row, using the instructions for the picot edge variation in chapter two, page 21.

3. Now it's time to attach the bar pin finding and outer backing to the cabochon. Follow steps 2 through 6 of the "Attaching Bar Pin Findings" section, starting on page 123, in the Appendix. Be sure to use the sheet metal flashing as directed to reinforce the attachment.

4. Trim the outer backing just inside the edge of the beadwork.

5. Next, stitch the cabochon's beaded edge to the under backing. Thread a needle with approximately 1 yard (.9 m) of beading thread (this technique is worked single-thread). From the back side at any point near the edge, stitch up through the outer backing. Leave a tail of approximately 9 inches (22.9 cm).

6. Stitch through the nearest picot bead above and then stitch up through the outer backing between the bead just stitched and the bead next to it. Pull to tighten.

7. Repeat step 6 all around the cabochon.

8. Bring the thread to the back side. Tie the tail thread and needle-end threads together with a square knot, weave in the ends, and cut. Congratulations; you've completed the pin!

creating your own designs

Once you've learned the basic techniques of beading with cabochons, the creative possibilities are unlimited. From that point on, it's all about applying your unique skills, experience, and imagination to make jewelry that is distinctly your own.

Indeed, one of the most fabulous things about beading with cabochons is that it allows you to make one-of-a-kind works. Each piece gains its uniqueness from the choices you make before you start and while you bead: the cabochon and beads you choose to use; the colors you select and the ways you combine them; the techniques you use and the sequence in which you apply them; and the design vision you have at the start and the adaptations you make to that vision as you complete the piece.

Choosing a Cabochon

Certainly, one of the first things to consider when formulating your design is the cabochon you want to use. It will be the focal point of your piece; its colors and surface characteristics will influence your design, including which beads you choose and their colors. In most cases, there will be no other cabochon just like it. This is true not only for dichroic glass and other artisan cabochons, but also for most natural stone cabochons such as jasper and agate.

Although it's obvious that the color of the cabochon will influence the design, it's equally important to consider the cabochon's shape and cut and their implications. As I mentioned in previous chapters, fat or chunky cabochons will require the use of certain bezel techniques to compensate for the edge cut. Likewise, small, delicate cabochons can be overwhelmed by large, fancy bezels and may need small beads and basic methods.

Considering Colors

Sometimes the colors in a cabochon can be difficult to match in a bead color and can present design challenges. One solution is to use a transparent bead that's close in color, and then select a thread color to help you alter the bead color. The bead's transparency will allow the thread color to show through and "mix" with that of the bead, thus adjusting the color to match more perfectly that of the cabochon. Another alternative is to select three or four beads, each a different color but all close to the color you want. Use one bead next to the other. In your finished creation, the colors of the beads will blend and create a new color effect.

Planning Ahead

There's more to design than just planning a piece's look; you also need to think about the techniques you'll use to achieve that look, and about how and when you'll apply those techniques. The order in which you perform the beading process's various steps can impact your design and make things easier or harder to do. If you're designing a brooch with an elaborate edge, for example, you'll need to plan to attach a pin finding before you stitch the final edge. If you're going to create a necklace, plan to add the necklace strand last, so that the strand doesn't get in the way while you're doing other, more detailed beadwork that requires you to turn the cabochon around or up or down.

In other instances, it's an issue of doing certain steps before others to make it easier to adjust your design as you go, so that you can create the most beautiful piece possible. If nothing else, experience has taught me that there is usually a difference between the design in my head versus the reality as I'm beading. Take the time to look at your creation as you're beading. Your plan is important, but you will often want to adjust and change it as you go. So if there are parts of the design that are very prominent, such as fringe, you may want to do those first to see whether, despite your plan, the reality needs to be adjusted—you may want to make your fringe longer or shorter, wider or narrower, for example.

Design Steps from Concept to Completion

Every project is different, but all share similar stages of development from beginning (an idea) to end (a finished piece of wonderful jewelry). Use the following steps as guidelines to help you through the entire process.

STEPS

1. Select a cabochon (see "Choosing a Cabochon," page 105).

2. Go bead shopping; review your entire bead "stash"; gather together all the beads, findings, and other materials you think you may want to use for the finished piece. This is an especially important step in cabochon beadwork. It'll not only help you conceive your overall design, but it can also help prevent problems later. For instance, at some point you may decide you want to introduce other colors or textures into the fringe or edge. If you've already made the basic beaded cabochon, it can be more difficult to incorporate new colors or materials or elements. Instead, consider all the possibilities from the beginning.

3. Consider your cabochon's shape and size. You'll want to select a method for beading the bezel that will accommodate your particular cabochon's properties. A large cabochon with a thick edge, for example, may require a bead-raised bezel. A small cabochon may need no bezel at all (see the sidebar).

Working with Small Cabochons

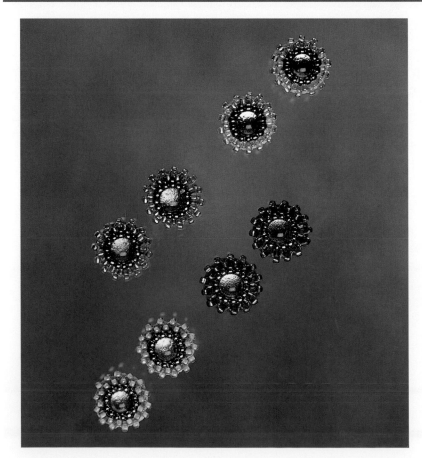

Cabochons that are very small (14 mm or less) can be used with great effect in your designs. If the cabochon is cut with a good slope from the dome to the edge, it's possible to eliminate the bezel row and use the basic base row to hold the stone in place. This is often desirable with small cabochons, because a bezel may cover too much of the cabochon. The key is to make the base row very snug around the cabochon, pulling tightly when stitching through the beads. The edge of the cabochon should slip under the bead edge (figure 1).

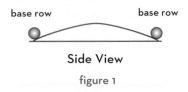

base row   base row

Side View

figure 1

4. Choose the beads that you want to use from the possibilities you considered in step 2, taking into account the bezel method you determined in step 3.

5. Plan your overall design, including which edge techniques and attachment methods you want to use. Again, coordinate this with your chosen beads, making sure that the choices you've made for beads and techniques are compatible. For instance, if you've decided to use a big, chunky bead for a necklace or bracelet strand, you wouldn't want to use the direct attachment method to join those beads to your basic beaded cabochon because they wouldn't lie properly when worn.

6. With your design planned, create the basic beaded cabochon. (If you're making earrings or a pin, remember to determine when to interrupt the steps for beading the basic cabochon, as discussed in the earrings and pins projects and in the Appendix on page 118, in order to attach the findings.)

7. If you've decided to use multiple cabochons (see page 110), join the cabochons together using the direct attachment method.

8. If you're creating a necklace or bracelet and are using an attachment method other than direct attachment, add the beads necessary for that attachment. For example, if you selected the turn bead method, now's the time to stitch on the turn beads. This will give you a clearer picture of how your design is working out, and it makes this part of the beading easier because there are no fringes or other beading to get tangled up in. Later, you'll add the actual necklace or bracelet strands.

9. Now it's time to bead the fringes in your design (if any). There can be a big difference between how your fringe looks in your plan versus reality. Creating the fringe now will allow you to make

adjustments easily to the lengths or numbers of fringes in your final design. For instance, you may have planned for 15 fringes (a center fringe and seven on each side), but once you see it, you may decide to expand to 19. Or perhaps you can see that you want to stop at 11 or 13. Since fringe is such a dominant part of the end design, do it early in the process so you can adjust it as desired.

10. Once you've completed any fringes (or if there are no fringes), you can add any other edge techniques you planned for your design.

11. Take a good look at your design; it's coming together nicely. If you need to add any other beading to your creation before you go on to the next step, do it now.

12. If you're making a necklace or bracelet, add the strands now. Attach any findings not yet added, such as clasps or ear wires.

13. You're finished! All that's left to do now is to wear your one-of-a-kind creation and dazzle the world!

Jewelry-Specific Design Tips

Necklaces, bracelets, earrings, pins: Whichever kind of beaded cabochon jewelry you decide to make, I hope that the following tips and advice help.

NECKLACES

Beaded cabochons lend themselves naturally to necklace designs. Often, because of changing fashions, the design challenge is not so much beading the cabochon itself, but determining how long to make the necklace strand.

There are standard necklace lengths, measured along the entire length of the necklace and including the clasp. Chokers, which need to be adjustable, are generally approximately 14 inches (35.6 cm) long.

Next is a short necklace of 16 inches (40.6cm). Other popular necklace lengths include 18- and 24-inch (45.7 and 61 cm) strands, and a long necklace of 36 inches (.9 m).

Generally, when waistlines in clothing fashions drop, as in tunic-style blouses, longer necklaces become more popular. When waistlines rise, such as with crop tops, shorter necklaces gain favor. And when strapless fashions become popular, chokers become the necklace length of choice.

One way to compensate for these fickle fashion trends and make your creation more timeless is to use an adjustable attachment. Make your necklace 17 to 18 inches (43.1 to 45.7 cm) long with the beadwork. On one side, use two jump rings to attach a hook-type clasp. On the other side, attach a chain that is approximately 5 inches (12.7 cm) long. You can then wear your creation short or long, whichever the current fashion dictates. This also lets you adjust the necklace to suit different outfits. For example, when wearing a blazer, you'd want the necklace shorter so that it would be visible in the V-neck of the collar. However, if you wore the same necklace with a sweater, you might want a longer length.

The beaded cabochon's design also can impact the choice of necklace length. For instance, a large, heavy pendant can be worn very comfortably, even on petite people, when the necklace strand is short, but it swings and bounces off the body when attached to a long strand.

BRACELETS

As you can see from the projects in this book, you can easily create a bracelet starting with a basic beaded cabochon. Just use the direct attachment method (page 47) and any of a variety of design configurations to add beads to both sides of the cabochon.

Round, oval, and other cabochon shapes make beautiful bracelets. Keep in mind, however, that most bracelet designs call for symmetry, so making them will be easiest when the count of edge beads is an even number. If the edge bead count is an odd number, your design will not be even and balanced. When this happens, you can "hide" the odd number of beads by using an edge stitch that doesn't have a repeating pattern. Use a raw edge (page24), turn bead edge (page 25), or ruffled edge (page 38) to make the difference less obvious. Or you can purposefully design the piece to have a creatively asymmetrical look.

EARRINGS

It is amazing how slight differences between two seemingly matched cabochons—minor variations in size, height, or slope—are magnified once you've added rows of beads or some fringe. To minimize this effect, try to choose cabochons that are as close to identical as possible in size, shape, and overall appearance. Likewise, it's important to bead the cabochons identically. This means keeping careful counts of the edge row beads on the first cabochon you bead so that you can duplicate the count on the other. For more details, see the sidebar (page 86) in the Double Cabochon Dangle Earrings project.

PINS AND BROOCHES

The important thing to remember when creating pins and brooches is that the cabochon itself—simply because of the look-at-me nature of a pin or brooch—is the star of the show, the inevitable focus point when worn. Keeping this in mind, you can achieve very dramatic effects by creating designs that play off the characteristics of the cabochon. Use fancy stones with lots of beads and fringe to create wonderful, funky pins, or combine solid-color cabochons with simple edge work to produce stylish, elegant brooches.

Other Design Considerations and Possibilities

Chances are, like most creative people, you'll start exploring ways to refine and expand your repertoire of techniques and designs as you gain experience with cabochons. Here are some possibilities.

USING OTHER STITCHES

The methods described in this book are based primarily on bead embroidery stitches that I've adapted specifically for cabochon beadwork. These stitches produce a clean, finished look and allow a great deal of variety in design. The techniques included also provide a way to create a bezel that will hold the cabochon in place while covering less of the cabochon than other methods. Still, other stitches, such as those that follow, can be used effectively. I mention them here only briefly as possibilities to consider; please refer to any good beading book for comprehensive how-to details.

Peyote Stitch

One of the other stitches often used to bead a cabochon is the peyote stitch. To create a bezel with this stitch, simply sew a row of beads onto the under backing around the cabochon, spacing the beads so that there is one bead's width between them (figure 2).

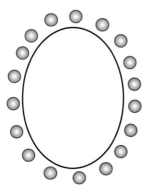

figure 2

For the second and subsequent rows, stitch through the beads in the previous row while adding a bead to each space (figure 3). Stitch rows as needed up toward the center of the cabochon, reducing the number of beads in each row as needed to fit (figure 4). The resulting bezel will have a zigzag appearance.

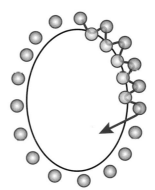

figure 3

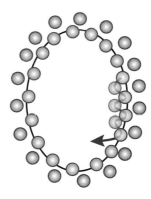

figure 4

Netting Stitches

Netting stitches are sometimes used to bead around cabochons. They're especially effective when you're creating an object, such as a sun catcher, that doesn't have a backing. There are many techniques for various kinds of netting stitches; most are fairly simple. You'll find instructions in beading books.

MULTIPLE CABOCHONS

As you can see from the photos here, combining several cabochons in a single piece produces a rich, dramatic look. There are basically two ways to accomplish this. One method is to create various basic beaded cabochons and then use the direct attachment method to join them together. Simply stitch the edge row from one cabochon directly to the edge row of a second cabochon. Or you can add beads in between the edge beads to increase the distance between the cabochons or to fill in gaps. Add as many cabochons as your design and heart desire. You can leave the gaps between the cabochons open, as in the necklace shown on the left above, or fill in the spaces with beads to produce the look of a solid surface, as in the necklace shown on the right above.

The second method involves applying various cabochons to the same backing. On a large piece of backing, draw an outline of what you want your final edge to be. Then mark where you want to place the cabochons and any other particular elements. Glue the cabochons to the backing one at a time, stitching the base and bezel rows before adding the next cabochon. It's usually best to add the largest cabochon first and proceed to the smallest last. Once you have all your cabochons on, fill in the spaces between the cabochons with other beadwork. When your beading nears the edges you marked when you started, cut around the outline (adjusting as necessary to fit the actual beadwork) before you sew on the final outside beading and/or rows.

Choose whichever method best fits your design. In general, the second method works nicely if your design is small to medium size. However, if your design is large, the first method may be preferable because it produces a piece that is more flexible, and thus more comfortable to wear.

USING OTHER OBJECTS

Once you become comfortable with applying the stitches in this book to standard cabochons, you can expand your horizons by widening your definition of "cabochon" to other objects. For example, large chunky beads can be used in place of a cabochon to create beautiful work. You can use the hole in the bead to sew into the under backing and thereby construct a firm base. Your design is then freed from the practical considerations of the bezel row because the stitches will hold the bead in place.

Many nuggets—irregular, polished stones such as quartz, turquoise, opal, and others, available through beading retailers—can make beautiful cabochon beadwork. When choosing a nugget, select one that has a side flat enough to glue to the under backing, and consider whether the cut of the nugget will provide a slope or other physical aspect that will allow you to create a bezel in which to hold the nugget. Or you can compensate by applying heavy-duty adhesive to glue the stone to the under backing and by using one of the raised bezel stitches.

BACKING YOUR WORK

One of the tests of true quality in any needlework, including beadwork, is the appearance of the back of the work. A piece with a neat, clean-looking back is considered higher quality. Cabochons have a flat back surface, so producing a smooth, finished look on the back is relatively easy and mostly a matter of applying skill and care as you stitch. The challenge is often greater with other objects, such as beads or nuggets, and with pieces that have many bead rows extending around the cabochon. To compensate for this, cut a piece of milk-jug plastic slightly smaller than the trimmed under backing and glue the plastic to the under backing before adding the outer backing. The plastic will give the beadwork a smooth, flat back surface.

BACKING TRANSPARENT CABOCHONS

Some cabochons have a degree of transparency in the glass or stone. However, unless you are creating something to hang in space, the cabochon will be lying on clothing or skin and the transparency will not be apparent. Accordingly, it is better to control the appearance by applying a backing to the cabochon. Before gluing such a cabochon to the under backing, try placing the cabochon on various colors of paper or other materials such as textiles or foils. Select the backing that creates the look you want and glue the cabochon to it; then trim that backing before adding the under backing.

Be Flexible, Have Fun

Always remember to be flexible when you're designing and creating cabochon beadwork. You may start out with a very specific design in mind, but as you work you'll often need to adjust your design to compensate for issues that arise: balance, weight, size, and more. For example, perhaps you have in mind a design that calls for a particular edge with a pattern that's repeated every four beads—but then you discover that the number of beads on the edge row isn't divisible by four. You'll have to look for a different solution. Being flexible, and understanding and using the techniques in this book, will help you deal with such issues.

Be sure, too, to consider all the elements in your final piece—not only individually, but also together. The best designs are balanced and complete, so look at your design as a whole. For example, necklaces with large, bold cabochon designs need large, bold necklace strands. If the necklace strand looks like an afterthought, the beauty of the entire piece is diminished. Likewise, a beautifully beaded cabochon pendant can be lost on a necklace strand that is overwhelming.

Above all, have fun! Play with unusual color combinations suggested by the cabochon's coloring, or try subtle, monochromatic color palettes. Combine different bead sizes, shapes, and textures. Think about other forms of beaded cabochon jewelry that you might create, such as rings or barrettes. Designing with cabochons is your opportunity to let your talents and creativity run free. Now's the time to take the bead stitching techniques you've learned and mastered here and use them to explore the unlimited possibilities that exist within your own imagination.

JAMIE CLOUD EAKIN,
Untitled, 2004,
Overall 19 inches (48.3 cm),
serpentine cabochon, seed beads
glass beads, serpentine beads,
freshwater pearls

SIS MORRIS,
Mermaid's Lair Necklace, 2004,
Overall 14 inches (35.6 cm),
mermaid dichroic cabochon,
seed beads, shells, sea urchin
spines, Swarovski crystal,
mother-of-pearl, silver fish,
blue fiber-optic glass

YVONNE CABALONA,
Blue Hawaii Necklace, 2004,
Overall 11 inches (27.9 cm),
paua shell cabochon, seed
beads, glass beads, hematite
beads, paua leaves

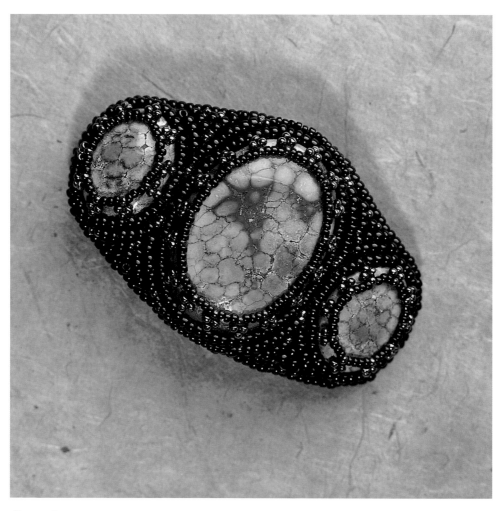

CATHIE SCHULTZE,
Untitled barrette, 2004,
Overall 3 inches (7.6 cm),
turquoise cabochon,
seed beads

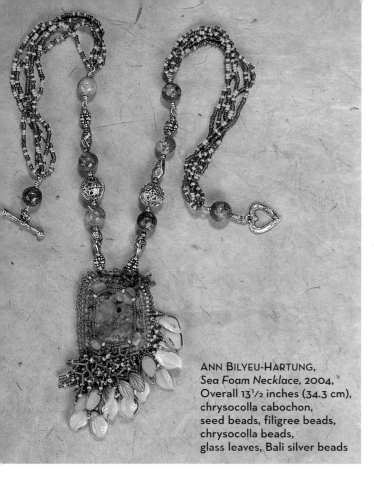

ANN BILYEU-HARTUNG,
Sea Foam Necklace, 2004,
Overall 13½ inches (34.3 cm),
chrysocolla cabochon,
seed beads, filigree beads,
chrysocolla beads,
glass leaves, Bali silver beads

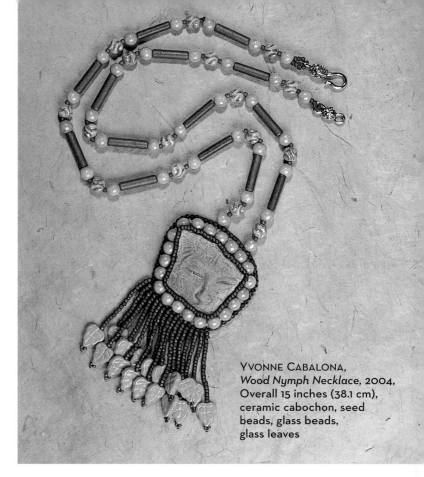

YVONNE CABALONA,
Wood Nymph Necklace, 2004,
Overall 15 inches (38.1 cm),
ceramic cabochon, seed
beads, glass beads,
glass leaves

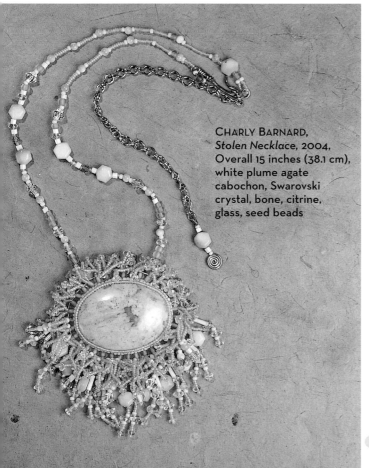

CHARLY BARNARD,
Stolen Necklace, 2004,
Overall 15 inches (38.1 cm),
white plume agate
cabochon, Swarovski
crystal, bone, citrine,
glass, seed beads

YVONNE CABALONA,
Contentment Necklace, 2004,
Overall 12½ inches (31.8 cm),
carved-bone cabochon, seed
beads, freshwater pearls

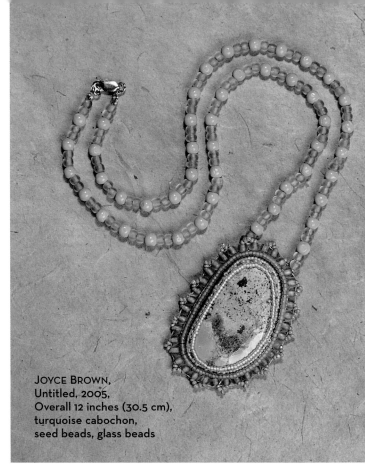

LEE WILKINS,
Pele Necklace, 2004,
Overall 11½ inches (29.2 cm),
petrified wood cabochon,
Swarovski crystal,
seed beads

JOYCE BROWN,
Untitled, 2005,
Overall 12 inches (30.5 cm),
turquoise cabochon,
seed beads, glass beads

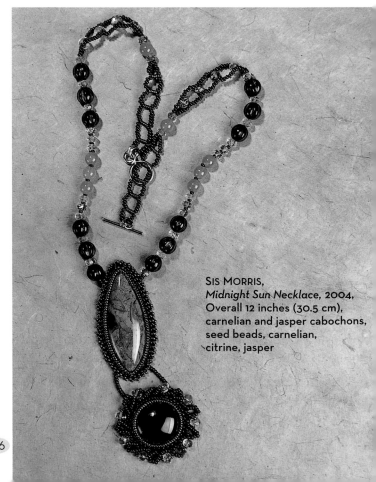

LEE WILKINS,
Untitled, 2005,
Overall 13 inches (33 cm),
snowflake obsidian cabochon,
seed beads, snowflake obsidian

SIS MORRIS,
Midnight Sun Necklace, 2004,
Overall 12 inches (30.5 cm),
carnelian and jasper cabochons,
seed beads, carnelian,
citrine, jasper

LEE WILKINS,
Untitled, 2005,
Overall 10 inches (25.4 cm),
leopardskin jasper cabochon,
seed beads, jasper

attaching findings

A creatively designed and skillfully executed beaded cabochon is an object of beauty all by itself. But most often you'll want to use that beautiful cabochon to make wonderful jewelry—and inevitably that requires attaching findings to your beadwork.

Because each project is different, you'll need to decide which kinds of findings are best for a particular piece, and which attachment technique is most suitable. Your choices will be influenced by the shape, size, and nature of the cabochon you're going to use and the beadwork you have planned for your design.

Necklaces and Bracelets

If you have a very long necklace design, you may not need to attach a finding—you can simply bead a continuous strand and slip the necklace over your head to wear it. In most cases, though, necklaces and bracelets need a clasp of some kind to allow putting them on and taking them off.

ATTACHING CLASPS

Nearly all clasp findings have a small eyelet for attaching them. You can sew the finding directly into your beadwork by stitching through the eyelet. However, as you've probably noticed if you've read or done any of the bracelet or necklace projects in this book, I prefer creating a loop at the end of the strand of the necklace or bracelet and then attaching the findings with jump rings.

This allows you to easily replace or change the finding later. If your finding breaks, you can simply put a new one on. This is also useful for changes you may want to make if you later decide to give your creation as a gift. It allows you to change the length and style of the clasp more easily and therefore the length of the necklace or bracelet.

To attach a jump ring, simply open the ring using two pairs of pliers as described on page 12, slip the ring over the loop and through the finding's eyelet, and then close it. To make doubly sure of a strong, secure connection, use two jump rings instead of just one.

Earrings

Earring findings come in a vast variety of styles, but fall into two basic categories: wire or clip findings for dangle earrings, and post findings for button earrings.

ATTACHING WIRES OR CLIPS FOR DANGLE EARRINGS

To attach wire or clip-style findings for dangle earrings, follow the steps in chapter two (page 15) for creating a basic beaded cabochon, then attach the earring findings using the instructions below. Once the findings are attached, complete the earrings by adding fringe and other edge techniques as desired for your design.

Instructions

1. Thread a needle with approximately 1 yard (.9 m) of beading thread (this technique is worked single-thread).

2. From the back side, stitch up through the backings under a selected edge bead, staying approximately 1/16 inch (1.6 mm) from the edge of the backing. Leave a tail approximately 9 inches (22.9 cm) long.

3. Stitch up through the edge bead.

4. Pick up three beads, string on the earring finding, and then add three more beads (figure 1).

finding

figure 1

5. Stitch down through the next edge bead (or one or two beads over, depending on how wide the loop is in your design), staying on the back side.

6. Stitch up through the backings to the top side, approximately 1/16 inch (1.6 mm) from the edge.

7. Stitch back up through the same edge bead and the added beads and finding, back to the original edge bead.

8. Stitch down through the original edge bead, staying on the back side.

9. Stitch up through the backings again to the top side.

10. Stitch through the edge bead and the added beads and findings back to the other edge bead. There are now three threads through the beads. Usually this is sufficient. However, if you have a heavy earring, you can repeat this stitching process until there are four or more threads in the loop.

11. To finish, stitch through the edge bead, staying on the top side. Stitch through the backings to the back side. If necessary, use a running stitch to stitch over to the tail thread. Tie the threads with a square knot, weave in the ends, and cut.

ATTACHING POST FINDINGS FOR BUTTON EARRINGS

Post findings for button earrings come in two pieces: a post pad, which has a vertical post on a flat metal base and looks a bit like a thumbtack, and a buttonlike closure that slips over the post to hold the earring in place on your ear (see the photo on page 13). Attaching a pad to a cabochon is a fairly simple matter—the key is knowing when, in the process of beading a basic cabochon, to interrupt the steps and attach the finding. In some cases, you can bead the entire cabochon first on the under backing only, then add the post pad and outer backing, and stitch the edge to the backing. That approach is generally limited, however, to designs that call for very small cabochons (7 mm or less) and/or that have only a basic picot edge. The instructions below describe the most versatile method—generally the best choice for designs that include fringe or almost any other detailed edge technique—in which you attach the finding before beading the cabochon's edge.

Instructions

1. Follow the instructions for creating a basic beaded cabochon in chapter two (page 15) through step 3. Then trim the under backing as described in part A of chapter two's step 4 (page 19). *Do not go on to attach the outer backing yet.*

2. Now it's time to glue the post pad to the cabochon's under backing. If you're using a small cabochon (10 mm or less), simply glue the post pad in place on the cabochon using heavy-duty adhesive, and proceed to step 7; the attachment will be sufficiently strong. If the cabochon is larger than 10 mm, you'll need to reinforce the attachment by adding a plastic backing over the post pad, between the under backing and the outer backing, following steps 3 through 6. In effect, this increases the size of the post pad and creates a secure attachment that's glued to the entire surface area of the cabochon's back.

3. Place the trimmed cabochon back side down on a flat piece of plastic cut from an empty milk jug. Using a marker, trace around the cabochon, marking its outline on the plastic. Then remove the cabochon and draw a second line approximately ⅛ inch (3 mm) inside of the traced line. Use scissors to cut the plastic on the new line.

4. Put the cut plastic on the back side of the cabochon; it should fit in the center with approximately ⅛ inch (3 mm) of under backing exposed all around the edge (figure 2). Trim the piece, if necessary. Position the post where you want it on the cabochon—make sure the pad will be completely covered by the plastic—and mark the pad's center, the point where the post will extend outward. (The illustration shows proper placement on the oval cabochon used in the Fringed Tiger-Eye Cabochon Earrings project on page 99.) Punch a hole in the plastic to accommodate the post. An old sewing machine needle works nicely for this.

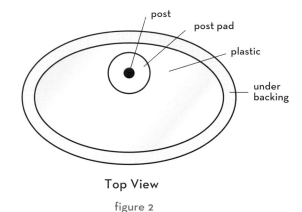

Top View

figure 2

5. Using a small amount of heavy-duty adhesive, attach the post pad to the plastic (figure 3).

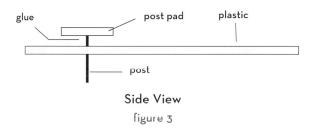

Side View

figure 3

6. After the glue has dried, spread heavy-duty adhesive over the back surface of the pin pad and the plastic and then attach the post pad and plastic to the cabochon's under backing (figure 4).

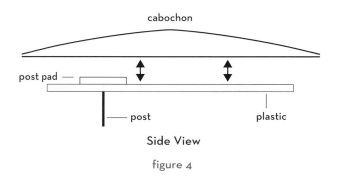

Side View

figure 4

7. When all the glue has dried completely, you can resume following the steps for the basic beaded cabochon, starting with part B of step 4 ("Attach the Outer Backing") on page 19. Generally, you will need to cut holes in the outer backing to accommodate the post finding. Use flexible glue to attach the outer backing.

8. Apply the edge row and finish the cabochon as desired for your design.

Another Option: Attach Findings Directly

Probably the most secure way to attach glue-on earring and pin findings to a cabochon is to glue the finding directly to the cabochon before adding an under backing or doing any beading. Just position the finding where you want it and apply an epoxy adhesive designed specifically for use on metal, stone, and/or glass.

This method is simple and provides an extremely strong connection, but it also has some drawbacks. Because both the under backing and the outer backing will go on top of it, the finding has to be tall enough to accommodate two layers of backing and still function properly. Earring findings with extra-long posts are available for this purpose. Average-size findings, however, may not be sufficient.

Also, because gluing a finding directly to a cabochon requires a finding smaller than the cabochon itself, the finished piece—which can be much larger after adding several rows of beads and/or lots of edge work—often needs a stronger attachment than the relatively small finding can provide. This can be a problem particularly if you're using small cabochons; this method is not suitable for them.

Finally, there's a practical problem with direct attachment that can take some of the fun out of beading with cabochons: Thread tends to get tangled in the finding as you sew on the beads.

Attaching findings directly to the cabochon can be a viable option, however, for certain projects that require an especially secure attachment. Every new project is different and presents its own set of conditions, so don't forget to keep direct attachment in your "tool box" of possible methods.

Pins

Adding a pin finding instantly transforms a solitary beaded cabochon into a piece of handcrafted jewelry.

ATTACHING TIE-TACK-STYLE AND STICKPIN FINDINGS

Tie-tack-style and stickpin findings make entirely different kinds of pins, but each has a post in the middle of a flat pad, much like post findings for earrings. In fact, you can use essentially the same methods for attaching these findings that you use for attaching earring post findings.

Here again, the key decision to make when attaching this type of pin finding is determining when, in the process of beading a basic cabochon, to interrupt the steps and attach the finding. In cases where the cabochon is very small and/or has only a basic picot edge, you can bead the entire cabochon first on the under backing only, then add the post pad and outer backing, and stitch the edge to the backing. In instances where the design calls for fringe or some other edge detail, it's best to attach the finding *before* beading the edge, as described here.

Instructions

1. Follow the instructions for creating a basic beaded cabochon in chapter two (page 15) through step 3. Then trim the under backing as described in part A of chapter two's step 4 (page 19). *Do not go on to attach the outer backing yet.*

2. Follow steps 2 through 7 in the "Attaching Post Findings for Button Earrings" section on page 120, substituting the pin finding for the earring finding and positioning the post pad appropriately for your pin design.

3. After you've attached the pin's outer backing over the plastic and allowed the flexible glue to dry, add the edge row and any other details needed to complete the design.

ATTACHING BAR PIN FINDINGS

Bar pin findings are available in many lengths, which makes them useful for a variety of cabochon shapes and sizes. This is the best kind of finding to use for larger pin designs or designs that are too heavy for tie-tack-style or stickpin findings. Another advantage of using a bar pin finding is that you can string a chain or cord through the pin finding and quickly turn your pin into a necklace.

Although you can glue a bar pin finding directly to a cabochon (see the sidebar on page 122), I recommend the technique described in steps 2 through 7 below, in which you glue a piece of metal to the beaded cabochon's under backing and then attach the finding before adding the outer backing. (I like to use thin sheet metal called "flashing," typically used in roofing, heating, and air conditioning. It's inexpensive, is widely available at hardware stores and home centers, and cuts easily with tin snips or heavy-duty scissors.) This method has several advantages: It allows you to use a larger pin finding than is possible with the direct glue method, it doesn't require extra-tall pin stems (any pin finding will work nicely), and the added metal provides a solid backing and a more stable pin.

Again, the main decision you have to make is *when* to attach the bar pin (and metal) as you bead the cabochon. The same principle holds true for bar pins as it does for tie-tack-style findings: If the cabochon is very small or has only a basic picot edge, you can bead the entire cabochon first on the under

backing only, then add the bar pin and outer backing, and stitch the edge to the backing. This is the case, for instance, with the Crazy Lace Agate Pin project on page 102; see that project for more details. In instances where the design calls for fringe or any other edge technique, it's best to attach the finding *before* beading the edge, as explained in the following instructions.

Instructions

1. Follow the instructions for creating a basic beaded cabochon in chapter two (page 15) through step 3. Then trim the under backing as described in part A of chapter two's step 4 (page 19). *Do not go on to attach the outer backing yet.*

2. Now you'll provide a strong base for the bar pin finding by gluing a layer of metal to the under backing. Put the beaded cabochon back side down on a piece of paper and trace its outline using a marker. Then remove the cabochon and draw a second line approximately ¼ inch (6 mm) inside of the traced line. Use scissors to cut out the pattern. Then put the pattern on the piece of metal and transfer the outline, using a marker. See photo A.

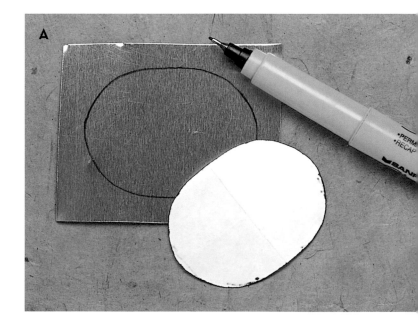

3. Using heavy-duty scissors or tin snips, cut around the outline. Place the cut metal on the back side of the cabochon; it should fit in the center with approximately ¼ inch (6 mm) of under backing exposed all around the edge. Trim the piece as needed. Then, using heavy-duty adhesive, glue the metal to the back side of the cabochon. See photo B.

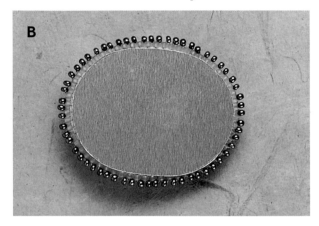

4. After the glue from the previous step has dried, glue the pin finding to the metal, again using heavy-duty adhesive. See photo C. Allow the glue to dry completely.

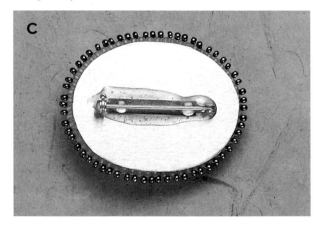

5. Lay a piece of outer backing material flat over the finding and cabochon and mark the points where the pin stems are. Cut small holes at the marks. See photo D.

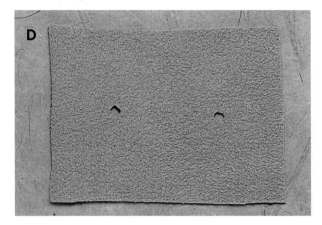

6. Spread a thin film of heavy-duty adhesive over the entire metal area, slip the pin and pin stems through the holes in the outer backing material, and press the outer backing down flat against the metal. See photo E. Allow the glue to dry completely.

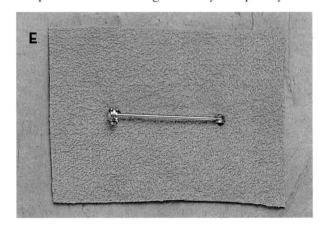

7. Trim the outer backing as described in the steps for the basic beaded cabochon, part B of step 4 on page 19.

8. Now you can finish beading the cabochon by creating the basic edge, as described in chapter two's step 5 (page 20), and adding any fringe or other edge techniques called for in your design.

Back side bead attachment, 53
Backstitch, four-six, 16
Backstitch, four-two, 18
Basic edge, 20
Bead-raised bezel, 61
Brick stitch, 35
Couch stitch, 62
Diamond bezel, 68
Direct attachment, 47
Fringe, 44
Knot, one-thread, 10
Knot, square, 10
Ladder stitch, top bail attachment, 55
Ladder stitch, two needle, 82
Lifted turned bead edge, 27
Peyote stitch, 109

Picot bezel, 66
Picot edge, 21
Pointed edge, 29
Raw edge, 24
Ruffled edge, 38
Running stitch, 37
Scalloped edge, 41
Star edge, 35
Top bail ladder attachment, 55
Top loop attachment, 57
Turn bead attachment, 50
Turned bead edge, 25
Twisted edge, 32
Two-bead edge, 21
Window bezel, 64

A Note About Suppliers

Usually, the supplies you need for making the projects in Lark
books can be found at your local craft supply store, discount
mart, home improvement center, or retail shop relevant to
the topic of the book. Occasionally, however, you may need
to buy materials or tools from specialty suppliers. In order to
provide you with the most up-to-date information, we have
created a list of suppliers on our website, which we update on
a regular basis. Visit us at www.larkbooks.com, click on 'Craft
Supply Sources,' and then click on the relevant topic. You will
find numerous companies listed with their web address
and/or mailing address and phone number.